Contributions to Management Science

More information about this series at http://www.springer.com/series/1505

Stefano Garzella • Raffaele Fiorentino

Synergy Value and Strategic Management

Inside the Black Box of Mergers and Acquisitions

Springer

Stefano Garzella
University of Naples Parthenope
Naples, Italy

Raffaele Fiorentino
University of Naples Parthenope
Naples, Italy

ISSN 1431-1941 ISSN 2197-716X (electronic)
Contributions to Management Science
ISBN 978-3-319-40669-5 ISBN 978-3-319-40671-8 (eBook)
DOI 10.1007/978-3-319-40671-8

Library of Congress Control Number: 2016951861

Printed on acid-free paper

This Springer imprint is published by Springer Nature
The registered company is Springer International Publishing AG Switzerland

Preface

Synergy management is an important challenge for firms, advisors, and practitioners involved in mergers and acquisitions (M&A). Synergy plays a key role in mergers and acquisitions (M&A), first, in the decision-making process and, then, in the integration step. However, despite the synergy value is commonly regarded as one of the M&A success factors, scholars show that firms generally fail in the achievement of expected synergy. There is a lack of comprehensive models of synergy management in the literature: the assessment of synergy value is a "black box" for both scholars and practitioners. Our aim is to provide a comprehensive framework of synergy management by the integration of findings from prior research and several disciplines. This framework highlights the main dimensions of synergy management in mergers and acquisitions, the common pitfalls, and new models and tools to overcome these pitfalls. Therefore, the book, on one hand, enriches M&A literature and suggests insights for scholars and, on the other, provides guidelines for practitioners involved in synergy management.

These findings are the result of a complex research project, begun some years ago, developed through the literature analysis and empirical research discussed and shared with various academics and practitioners and colleagues and friends. Each of them has provided useful advice and suggestions.

Then, we would like first to acknowledge our colleagues of the Universities of Naples "Parthenope," Pisa, and Rome "La Sapienza" for useful exchange of views. We are also grateful to the members of the research project on "Growth Strategies, Corporate Governance Processes and Value Creation" funded by the PRIN Program of the Italian Minister of Education, Universities and Research. This study was also supported by the research funds of the University of Naples Parthenope. Finally, thanks to reviewers and participants to conferences and workshops where we discussed prior versions of this work for advice and insights.

Naples, Italy
April 2016

Stefano Garzella
Raffaele Fiorentino

Contents

Chapter 1
Introduction

Abstract There is a lack of comprehensive models of synergy management in the literature: the assessment of synergy value is a "black box" for both scholars and practitioners. Our aim is to provide a comprehensive framework of synergy management by the integration of findings from prior research and several disciplines. This framework highlights: the main dimensions of synergy management in mergers and acquisitions, the common pitfalls, and new models and tools to overcome these pitfalls.

In order to reach our aim we have articulated the book in three chapters analyzing: the role of synergy in M&As; the synergy assessment process; the management of synergy pitfalls.

Keywords Synergy • Pitfalls • Blackbox • Framework

Synergy is back at the top of the corporate agenda in M&A processes. However, the success of external growth strategies has been limited and the most recent deals do not show any meaningful difference with respect to M&A failure rates (Bruner 2004; Cartwright and Schoenberg 2006; Hitt et al. 2009; Thanos and Papadakis 2012). Unidentified mediators seem to drive variance in M&A performance (King et al. 2004).

Most of the deal's announcements with high synergy expectations are often followed by disappointing performance. Each M&A initiative embarks on the same enthusiastic quest for synergy achievement and faces the same challenges. Harding and Rovit (2005), building on the results of a research conducted by Bain & Company, affirmed that two-thirds of the executives responsible for acquisitions believe to have overestimated the synergic potential and underline the relevance of this error for the deal failure.

Consistently, the study of M&A is an established body of literature in management research (Bertini 1990; Collis and Montgomery 1997; Galeotti and Garzella 2013; Keil et al. 2013; Haleblian et al. 2009; Onesti et al. 2012; Porter 1980). M&A research, specifically in accounting and finance, largely focuses on value creation issues. However, published results are often divergent and measurements incomplete (e.g., Bruner 2002). For instance, although there is some evidence that M&A deals create short-term value for shareholders in target firms, the empirical support for the creation of long-term value in acquiring firms remains ambiguous (Agarwal

S. Garzella, R. Fiorentino, *Synergy Value and Strategic Management*,
Contributions to Management Science, DOI 10.1007/978-3-319-40671-8_1

and Jaffe 2000; Jensen and Ruback 1983). In the same vein, Bruner (2004) suggests the high difficulty of adopting strong measures suitable for assessing the outcomes of M&A deals, such as the difference between post-deal actual stock prices and potential stock prices if the operation had not been completed.

Prior research underlines the importance of the pre-acquisition phase, when the M&A's contribution to the overarching corporate strategy and its price are still under evaluation. One of the main challenges in M&A is developing a pre-acquisition decision process that indicates which acquisitions are "right", even under conditions of incomplete information, rapidity and secretiveness (Evans and Bishop 2001). In other words, to find true value-creating acquisitions, firms must avoid "false positive" acquisition opportunities that are generally accepted when they should have been rejected, but the M&A literature seldom focuses on this topic (Sirower 2003). This problem may become even more relevant if, as recent studies have highlighted (Zollo and Meier 2008), financial markets are unable to forecast the real performance of acquisitions from short-term returns. M&A deals, which are notorious for their difficulty of reversal and onerous absorption of financial resources, cannot be hasty and must be carefully considered and analysed.

Synergy play a key role in M&As. Synergy is one of the most important motives for M&A operations (Mukherjee et al. 2004). For example, Eccles et al. (1999: 136), emphasising that "many failures occur, though, simply because the acquiring company paid too much for the acquisition", suggest the inaccurate assessment of synergy as one of the possible reasons for M&A failures. In the assessment process, it is fundamental to assess the risks of a bad valuation of synergy (Copeland 1994; Haspeslagh and Jemison 1991; Rappaport and Sirower 1999). The value creation in M&A deals depends on both the value of synergy expectations and the effectiveness of the assessment process. Ambiguity of expectations represents one of the main decisional problems in M&A because "if there are no true synergies between the merging firms in the first place, then even to high quality, low-cost implementation of the merger may lead to only negligible benefits" (Zollo and Meier 2008: 60). In this respect, Sirower (1997) observes that synergies are often promised but seldom realised, albeit without reporting detailed findings on potential synergy assessment.

Over time, research on M&A success and failure has analyzed synergy with reference to many areas of investigation and several topics (Cartwright and Schoenberg 2006; Chatterjee 1986; Garzella 2006; Homburg and Bucerius 2006; Papadakis and Thanos 2010; Shaver 2006; Sirower 1997; Zaheer et al. 2013; Zhou 2011; Zollo and Meier 2008). Studies have defined the synergy concept as "the increase in performance of the combined firm over what the two firms are already expected or required to accomplish as independent firms" (Sirower 1997: 20). Many M&A frameworks utilize the degree of synergy realization as a measure of a deal's success (Larsson and Finkelstein 1999). Similarly, a lack of synergy value and a realized synergy that is valued lower than its potential are measures of M&A failure. Indeed, the value difference between synergy realization and synergy expectations has been increasingly used to investigate M&A performance in empirical studies (Gates and Very 2003).

The assessment of the synergy value is regarded as one of the most critical points in M&A (Larsson and Finkelstein 1999), and the relative usefulness of various company valuation models has been the subject of considerable empirical research in recent years (Barker 1999; Garzella and Fiorentino 2014; Lundholm and O'Keefe 2001; Penman 2001). These studies are often focused on a comparison of residual income-based accounting valuation models and DCF (discounted cash flows) models (Penman and Sougiannis 1998; Francis et al. 2000; Courteau et al. 2001). However, these theoretically equivalent valuation models (i.e., residual in-come and DCF) are sometimes compared to the relatively "unsophisticated" valuation models (i.e., multiples models) that are increasingly being used by practitioners (Imam et al. 2008). Aside from statistical association between equity valuations and share prices (Frankel and Lee 1998; Biddle et al. 1997), this phenomenon led to research on the actual practices of different types of experts (e.g., Arnold and Mozier 1984; Barker 1999; Block 1999; Burchell et al. 1980; Demirakos et al. 2004; Fiorentino and Garzella 2014).

Despite several studies on the practices of valuation models in M&A (Baker et al. 1981; Mukherjee et al. 2004; Villalonga 2004) and on theoretical models suggesting that the autonomous assessment of synergy does exist (Damodaran 2005; Galeotti 1995; Kode et al. 2003; Rappaport 1986), the practices of synergy valuation models in M&A are surprisingly overlooked in empirical research. Indeed, scholars have failed to identify factors that meaningfully influence the M&A failure rate (Cartwright and Schoenberg 2006). Notwithstanding an intense debate in the literature on this topic (e.g., Bruner 2004; Martinez-Jerez 2008; Zollo and Meier 2008), theoretical and empirical research still lacks a common understanding of the effectiveness of synergy management in M&A. Management studies do not offer a comprehensive overview of synergies and there are few broad research on risks relating to their assessment and realization (Goold and Campbell 1998; Fiorentino and Garzella 2015).

Accordingly, further studies are needed. The literature has searched for critical success factors in M&A, but there are few studies on its pitfalls (Gomes et al. 2013), Although the existing body of knowledge in prior M&A research marginally considers the "managing" perspective of synergy (Larsson and Finkelstein 1999; Lietdka 1998; Zollo and Meier 2008), the synergy background remains fragmented and the divergent assumptions and results have particularly strong implications for managers' commitment to synergy (Haleblian et al. 2009; Knudsen 2003). The process approach, recommended by many scholars, has not been developed as expected, and prior studies tend to focus on either post-acquisition management or pre-deal analysis (Hayward 2002).

As a consequence, it is necessary to develop a comprehensive framework focused on synergy, based on a "managing" perspective that examines the entire M&A process, able to integrate the findings of several literature streams in a multidisciplinary view, and useful to business practitioners (Ernst and Young 2014; Roland Berger 2011). Put simply, the process of planning and strategic analysis builds on the assessment of synergies, which therefore demands effective models and tools (Colombo et al. 2007; Kode et al. 2003). As Evans and Bishop (2001: 83) argue, "Synergies must not be mythical. They must be hardly contested, accurately forecasted, and appropriately discounted net cash flows that reflect their probability of success under carefully constructed and reviewed time schedules". Thus, the key question is how synergies should be evaluated and how firms may avoid risks of potential synergy misassessment (Damodaran 2005). Therefore, it is also necessary to extend previous models to further the assessment of synergy expectations in the pre-acquisition phase of M&A agreements, which are a key element for the success of M&A deals (KPMG 1999).

There is a lack of comprehensive models of synergy management in the literature: the assessment of synergy value is a "black box" for both scholars and practitioners. Our aim is to provide a comprehensive framework of synergy management by the integration of findings from prior research and several disciplines. This framework highlights: the main dimensions of synergy management in mergers and acquisitions, the common pitfalls, and new models and tools to overcome these pitfalls.

In order to reach our aim we have articulated the book in three chapters analyzing: the role of synergy in M&As; the synergy assessment process; the management of synergy pitfalls.

The first chapter begins with a review of synergy management in M&A literature. We introduce concepts such as strategic management and growth strategies in order to facilitate the analysis of synergy in M&As. Later, we compile a comprehensive overview of synergy management in M&A.

In the second chapter, we analyze the synergy assessment process with reference to both the quantitative and the qualitative perspectives. We first review the main synergy valuation models; second, we investigate the strategic factors to analyze in the synergy assessment; third, we advance a framework proposal for the synergy assessment process to avoid common mistakes in M&A.

In the third chapter, we analyze three synergy pitfalls that may hinder M&A success. These pitfalls include: the mirage, the gravity hill, and amnesia. Then we categorize the most relevant dimensions of synergy pitfalls management: the steps of the M&A process; the several values of synergy; the forbidding effects of an improper approach to synergy management; the potential causes of synergy trap; and the practical solutions to synergy pitfalls. Based on the combination of these dimensions, we develop a conceptual framework. Finally, we advance practical solutions to avoid or limit these pitfalls. Over prior tools and actions, we propose a synergy statement, a multidimensional chart who may help researchers and practitioners to understand what is the overall amount of synergy.

References

Agarwal A, Jaffe JF (2000) The post-merger performance puzzle. In: Cooper C, Gregory A (eds) Advances in mergers and acquisitions, vol 1. Elsevier, New York, NY, pp 7–14
Arnold JA, Mozier P (1984) A survey of the methods used by UK investments analysts to appraise investments in ordinary shares. Account Bus Res 14(55):195–207
Baker HK, Miller TO, Ramsperger BJ (1981) An inside look at corporate mergers and acquisitions. MSU Bus Top 29(1):49–57
Barker RG (1999) The role of dividends in valuation models used by analysts and fund managers. Eur Account Rev 8(2):195–218
Bertini U (1990) Scritti di politica aziendale. Giappichelli, Torino
Biddle GC, Bowen RM, Wallace JS (1997) Does EVA® beat earnings? Evidence on associations with stock returns and firm values. J Account Econ 24(3):301–336
Block SB (1999) A study of financial analysts: practice and theory. Financ Anal Journal 55(4): 86–95
Bruner RF (2002) Does M&A pay? A survey of evidence for the decision maker. J Appl Finance Theory Pract Educ 12(1):48–88
Bruner RF (2004) Deals from hell: M&A lessons that rise above the ashes. Wiley, New York, NY
Burchell S, Clubb C, Hopwood A, Hughes J, Nahapiet J (1980) The roles of accounting in organizations and society. Acc Organ Soc 5:5–27
Cartwright S, Schoenberg R (2006) Thirty years of mergers and acquisitions research: recent advances and future opportunities. Br J Manag 17(S1):s1–s5
Chatterjee S (1986) Types of synergy and economic value: the impact of acquisitions on merging and rival firms. Strateg Manag J 7(2):119–139
Collis DJ, Montgomery CA (1997) Corporate strategy. McGraw-Hill, New York, NY
Colombo G, Conca V, Buongiorno M, Gnan L (2007) Integrating cross-border acquisitions: a process-oriented approach. Long Range Plan 40(2):202–222
Copeland T (1994) Why value value? McKinsey Q 4:97–109
Courteau L, Kao J, Richardson G (2001) Equity valuation employing the ideal versus ad hoc terminal value expressions. Contemp Account Res 18(4):625–661
Damodaran A (2005) The value of synergy. Stern School of Business, New York, October 30, 2005. SSRN 841486(2005)
Demirakos EG, Strong N, Walker M (2004) What valuation models do analysts use? Account Horiz 18(4):221–240
Eccles RG, Lanes KL, Wilson TC (1999) Are you paying too much for that acquisition? Harv Bus Rev 77(4):136–146
Ernst and Young (2014) How much synergy do you need? www.ey.com
Evans FC, Bishop DM (2001) Valuation for M&A: building value in private companies. Wiley, New York, NY
Fiorentino R, Garzella S (2014) The synergy valuation models: towards the real value of mergers and acquisitions. Int Res J Financ Econ 124:71–82
Fiorentino R, Garzella S (2015) Synergy pitfalls management in mergers and acquisitions. Manag Decis 53(7):1469–1501
Francis J, Olsson P, Oswald D (2000) Comparing the accuracy and explainability of dividend, free cash flow, and abnormal earnings equity value estimates. J Account Res 38(1):45–70
Frankel R, Lee CMC (1998) Accounting valuation, market expectations, and cross-sectional stock returns. J Account Econ 25(3):283–319
Galeotti M (1995) La valutazione strategica nell'ipotesi di cessione dell'azienda. Giuffré, Milano
Galeotti M, Garzella S (2013) Governo strategico dell'azienda. Giappichelli, Torino
Garzella S (2006) Il governo delle sinergie. Giappichelli, Torino
Garzella S, Fiorentino R (2014) A synergy measurement model to support the pre-deal decision making in mergers and acquisitions. Manag Decis 52(6):1194–1216

Gates S, Very P (2003) Measuring performance during M&A integration. Long Range Plan 36(2): 167–186
Gomes E, Angwin DN, Weber Y, Tarba SY (2013) Critical success factors through the mergers and acquisitions process: revealing pre- and post-M&A connections for improved performance. Thunderbird Int Bus Rev 55(1):13–35
Goold M, Campbell A (1998) Desperately seeking synergy. Harv Bus Rev 76:131–143
Haleblian J, Devers C, McNamara G, Carpenter M, Davison R (2009) Taking stock of what we know about mergers and acquisitions: a review and research agenda. J Manag 35(3):469–502
Harding D, Rovit S (2005) Mastering the merger: four critical decisions that make or break the deal. Harvard Business School Press, Boston, MA
Haspeslagh PC, Jemison DB (1991) Managing acquisitions. Free Press, New York
Hayward MLA (2002) When do firms learn from their acquisition experience? Evidence from 1990-1995. Strateg Manag J 23(1):21–39
Hitt M, King D, Kriishnan H, Makri M, Schijven K, Zhu H (2009) Mergers and acquisitions: overcoming pitfalls, building synergy, and creating value. Bus Horiz 52(6):523–529
Homburg C, Bucerius M (2006) Is speed of integration really a success factor of mergers and acquisitions? An analysis of the role of internal and external relatedness. Strateg Manag J 27(4):347–367
Imam S, Barker R, Clubb C (2008) The use of valuation models by UK investment analysts. Eur Account Rev 17(3):503–535
Jensen MC, Ruback RS (1983) The market for corporate control: the scientific evidence. J Financ Econ 11(1–4):5–50
Keil T, Laamanen T, McGrath RG (2013) Is a counterattack the best defense? Competitive dynamics through acquisitions. Long Range Plan 46(3):195–215
King DR, Dalton DR, Daily CD, Covin JG (2004) Meta-analyses of post-acquisition performance: indications of unidentified moderators. Strateg Manag J 25(2):187–200
Knudsen C (2003) The essential tension in the social sciences: between the "unification" and "fragmentation" trap. Edward Elgar, Cheltenham, England
Kode GVM, Ford JC, Sutherland MM (2003) A conceptual model for evaluation of synergies in mergers and acquisitions. South Afr J Bus 48(1):27–38
KPMG (1999) Unlocking shareholder value: the keys to success. KPMG, London, UK
Larsson R, Finkelstein S (1999) Integrating strategic, organizational, and human resource perspectives on mergers and acquisitions: a case survey of synergy realization. Organ Sci 10(1): 1–26
Lietdka JM (1998) Synergy revisited: how a "Screwball Buzzword" can be good for the bottom line. Bus Strateg Rev 9(2):45–55
Lundholm RJ, O'Keefe T (2001) Reconciling value estimates from the discounted cash flow model and the residual income model. Contemp Account Res 18(2):311–335
Martinez-Jerez FA (2008) Governance and merger accounting: evidence from stock price reactions to purchase versus pooling. Eur Account Rev 17(1):5–35
Mukherjee TK, Kiymaz H, Baker K (2004) Merger motives and target valuation: a survey of evidence from CFOs. J Appl Financ 14(2):7–24
Onesti T, Angiola N, Bianchi Martini S, Garzella S, Muserra AL (2012) Strategie di sviluppo aziendale, processi di corporate governance e creazione di valore. Teorie, analisi empiriche ed esperienze a confronto. FrancoAngeli, MILANO
Papadakis VM, Thanos IC (2010) Measuring the performance of acquisitions: an empirical investigation using multiple criteria. Br J Manag 21:859–873
Penman SH (2001) On comparing cash flow and accrual models for use in equity valuation. Contemp Account Res 18(4):681–692
Penman SH, Sougiannis T (1998) A comparison of dividend, cash flow and earnings approach to equity valuation. Contemp Account Res 15(3):343–383
Porter ME (1980) Competitive strategy. Free Press, New York, NY

Rappaport A (1986) Creating shareholder value: the new standard for business performance. Free Press, New York, NY

Rappaport A, Sirower ML (1999) Stock or cash? The trade-offs for buyers and sellers in mergers and acquisitions. Harv Bus Rev 77(6):147–158

Roland Berger (2011) Synergy management for successful post merger integration. www.rolandberger.com

Shaver JM (2006) A paradox of synergy: contagion and capacity effects in mergers and acquisitions. Acad Manag Rev 31(4):962–976

Sirower ML (1997) Synergy trap: how companies lose the acquisition game. Simon & Schuster), New York, NY

Sirower ML (2003) Becoming a prepared acquirer. Eur Bus Forum 16:55–59

Thanos IC, Papadakis VM (2012) The use of accounting-based measures in measuring M&A performance: a review of five decades of research. In: Cooper CL, Finkelstein S (eds) Advances in mergers and acquisitions, vol 10. Emerald, Bingley, UK, pp 103–120

Villalonga B (2004) Diversification discount or premium? New evidence from the business tracking series. J Financ 42(2):943–963

Zaheer A, Castaner X, Souder R (2013) Synergy sources, target autonomy, and integration in acquisitions. J Manag 39(3):604–632

Zhou YM (2011) Synergy, coordination costs, and diversification choices. Strateg Manag J 32: 624–639

Zollo M, Meier D (2008) What is M&A performance? Acad Manag Perspect 22(3):55–77

Chapter 2
M&A Success and Failure: The Role of Synergy Management

Abstract This chapter introduces the role of synergy management in mergers and acquisitions (M&As). M&As have increasing attention in the external growth strategies of firms. Synergy plays a key role in M&As, first, in the decision making process and, then, in the performance evaluation. Prior studies have paradoxically regarded synergy. The "synergy hypothesis" stream considers synergy as the main motive of M&As. In contrast, the "synergy inflation" stream argues that synergy is the main failure's reason of M&A. Overall, prior research shows that synergy is an important motivation of M&As, has tended to be overestimated and has been difficult to achieve. Accordingly, we argue that synergy is not a "myth" and could improve the value of combined firms if managers and executive had able to develop an effective management avoiding hidden pitfalls.

Keywords Mergers • Acquisition • Success • Failure • Synergy • Risks

2.1 Strategic Management, Growth Strategies, and M&As

The strategic management affects the firm's success by the peculiar paths of growth. For this reason, before focusing on synergy management, the topic of this study, it is useful summarize the complex relations among strategic management, growth strategies and M&As. The organization of the elements and relationships is neither casual nor superordinate, but is the result of decisions made by the people who, with different roles and different responsibilities, are involved in the governance (Bertini 1995).

The firm is an open and interactive system that develops continuous relations with its external environment (Bertini 1990; Boulding 1981; Luhmann 1995). The firm is a social system with economic purpose. Specifically, the firm can be described as: a network of relationships with other players in the economic and social world; object and subject of expectations and demands; as an hub of complex flows of materials, information and financial outward; the node of needs and expectations, in many cases divergent (Bianchi Martini 2009; Galeotti and Garzella 2013).

S. Garzella, R. Fiorentino, *Synergy Value and Strategic Management*,
Contributions to Management Science, DOI 10.1007/978-3-319-40671-8_2

The system of relations with the environment has a key role in the strategic management of the firm (Aaker 2008; Abell 1980; Collis and Montgomery 1997). The firm's management needs a series of ongoing relationships with various external players (Freeman 1984; Hamel and Prahalad 2013; Porter 2008; Porter 1987):

(a) Suppliers, for procurement processes of resources;
(b) Customers, in order to sell products on the market;
(c) Competitors, as a result of competition in the market;
(d) The lenders, to cover the financing needs;
(e) The shareholders, with regard to the allocation and the remuneration of equity;
(f) Workers, individually and/or together in trade unions, in relation to their role in business processes;
(g) The social community, which includes all those institutions (government, public administration, and private organizations) that have relations with the firm.

Managers and executives should achieve a balanced relationship with the external players. Firm's success is based on a dynamic "harmony" between both the organizations structure and the economic and social system (external consonance), and the several firm sub-systems (internal harmony).

The strategic management may determine the basic characteristics of the interaction model between the firm and the external environment, as well as to realize the organizational structure to provide the best support to this process (Mintzberg et al. 2005; Normann 1977). Firms, in order to strengthen their profitability to achieve a competitive advantage, should continuously develop new growth strategies. The search for success pushes frequently towards M&As, partnerships and strategic alliances.

Studies from disciplines such as economics, strategic management, organizational behaviour and general management have focused on growth strategies by several approaches (Andrews 1971; Ansoff 1965; Mintzberg et al. 2005; Villalonga and McGahan 2005). Theories of the firm generally examine how firms choose whether to make or buy individual components (Coase 1937; Williamson 1975). The traditional theories in the study of growth strategies have involved transaction cost economics and resource-based views of the firm.

The transaction cost economics (TCE) analyse the properties of the transactions to find the main factors producing benefits and costs in hierarchy and market decisions (Williamson 1975). This theory accepts production costs as given and focuses on the governance benefits and costs of different growth decisions. Outsourcing can be risky due to lack of proprietary information, loss of control, and a low likelihood of gaining knowledge (Collis and Montgomery 1997). The main contribution of transaction cost economics is to specify the conditions under which firms should manage activities inside or outside.

Resource-based scholars analyse the firm as a system of distinctive resources and competences that can create competitive advantage (Barney 1991). In the resource-based view, firm decisions influence production costs and learning opportunities. Specifically, internal growth decisions provide cost reduction and future development ability. The main contribution of the resource-based view of the firm was to clarify the determinants of internal and external growth strategies. The traditional conclusion of these literature streams is that firms tend to manage activities through outsourcing choices when alternatives require higher investments (Coase 1937; Williamson 1975) or when external resources have substantial capability advantages (Barney 1999).

The findings of theories have influenced prior strategic management and growth strategies studies (e.g., Hitt et al. 2000; Holcomb and Hitt 2007; Vivek et al. 2008). Typically, scholars usually distinguish between the internal growth strategies and the external growth strategies (Guth 1980). When the development process is implemented without resources and capabilities of other organizations, firms follow internal growth strategies. Instead, external growth strategies are pursued by exploiting resource, knowledge and capabilities of other firms (Collis and Montgomery 1997; Hill et al. 2014; Rothaermel 2015). Despite of our focus on synergy on M&As, it is useful to systematically analyse the overall growth strategies paths.

According to the traditional distinction in internal growth and external growth, in internal growth strategies the firm acquires single elements which become part of the system only after their combination with prior firm's elements. The strategic plan is, in fact, pursued mainly by exploiting their distinctive competencies. The internal development strategies include a redefinition of relations and relationships between the elements in order to improve the synergy inside the firm and to strengthen the company's competitive position. The internal growth strategies are based on an internal entrepreneurship, on the one hand, and on the decisive contribution made by the management and the organizational structure, on the other.

This development is generally realized through entry strategies—the company uses the resources and internal capacity to enter into new industries—and horizontal concepts—the company uses the resources and internal capabilities to extend its competitive action without changing its competitive field.

Instead the external growth strategies are characterized by the combination of two or more firms. Firms realize external growth strategies by sharing their development path with paths of other organizations (Grant 2015; Thompson et al. 2013). Among the several types of combinations there are, on the one hand, the mergers and acquisitions requiring a huge amount of resources and a significant reorganization and behavioural change of involved firms and, on the other hand, strategic alliances characterized by informal agreements and a lower use of resources and a low impact on behaviours. Despite the specificity of the various types of agreements, the external growth strategies are essentially aimed at the pursuit of competitive advantage positions by a timing faster than internal growth strategies. The external growth strategies, in fact, should allow to competitive advantage as they allow the creation of so-called "economies of speed" in obtaining new resources and in to access to new markets. The importance of the time factor underlines the strategic importance of a growth process that allows the completion of the product range, geographical presence, as well as the completion of technology and the access to emerging technologies, minimizing the time.

The decision about what growth strategy to choose is very relevant, since the two traditional and "extreme" logics—internal development and external development—have advantages and disadvantages, in terms of speed, reversibility, information availability, and success probability, and in many cases the alternative paths are even antithetical and symmetrical: the strengths of a growth strategy are the weaknesses of the other, and vice versa.

For this reason in many cases firms search for intermediate strategies between the pure internal or external growth by pursuing the realization of informal agreements and strategic alliances (Cummings and Holmberg 2012). Because firms are increasingly making joint decisions for resource, knowledge and activities management due to synergies that stem from interrelated processes and activities (Foss 1996; Grant 2015; Parmigiani and Mitchell 2009; Santos and Eisenhardt 2005; Tortoriello and Krackhardt 2010), new arguments have emerged in the literature. [1]Transaction cost economics formerly argued that between the two ends of governance, integration and market, there are the firm's boundaries. The questioning on the value of "ownership" and recognition of potential benefits has come because the joint use of skills and knowledge has highlighted boundary management

[1]In order to thoroughly analyzing synergy management, it is useful to contextualize mergers and acquisitions in the growth strategies framework by showing the traditional benefits and disadvantages of each path. Specifically, the strengths and weaknesses emerging from prior studies can be summarized in the following tables:

Benefits	Disadvantages
Internal growth strategies	
Incremental development of decisions and evaluation process, with the possibility of consecutive conversion	Slowness
Coherent with firm resources and culture	Potential difficulties in internal resources development
To improve internal entrepreneurship	Traditionally increase industry competition
External growth strategies	
Synergies and possible access to resources difficult to replicate	Traditionally high integration costs and financial needs
Elimination of potential competitors	Risks of costs duplication
Quickly	Risks of organizational conflicts
Boundaries strategies	
Synergies and possible access to resources difficult to replicate	Difficult of integration
Highly flexible	No control
Quickly and limited cost	Slowness and waste of resources
Elimination of potential competitors	Facilitation for a potential competitor

(Alexander 1997). A relational or social network view has emerged in which the boundary concept is used to embrace resources and activities that can be controlled and influenced by the organization (Garzella 2000).

Boundary strategies emerge as third between the strengths of integration and the benefits of outsourcing (Hargadon 2002; McEvily and Zaheer 1999; Takeishi 2001). As a consequence the literature review posits that the management of resource, knowledge and activities push towards three main options, internal growth, external growth and boundaries growth, of combining resources to obtain and sustain competitive advantage (Dyer and Singh 1998; Garzella 2000).

The current market evolutions push firms to business combinations. The business combinations generally lead to: a radical change of the competitive forces in the involved industries; an overall rethinking in the organizational structure, in the governance, and in the business models of the firms.

The processes of external growth highlight two main interconnected dimensions of action and analysis, which are related to the communication provided to the markets from executives of the involved companies: the first dimension is the integration and reorganization process of firms; the second dimension addresses the value implications expected by the deals.

These deals by the combination of businesses, resources and organizational processes is strained, in most cases, to increase the competitiveness, and the financial results of firms. Value creation and financial results improvement are key indicators to analyze in a systematic and analytical way.

The business combination is a research topic that has attracted the attention of scholars over the years. However, the analysis of relations between the several implementation types leaves open questions for further researches. In particular, the literature review highlights, among other things, research opportunities on issues such as the analysis and evaluation of synergies.

The external growth processes can be realized, first, through mergers and acquisitions.

A synthetic overview on M&As is functional to better understanding the role of synergy management.

Mergers and acquisitions are deals by which a firm takes control, direct or indirect, of another firm. The combination of two or more companies is generally developed according to three main ways (Bruner 2004a, b; Galpin 2014; Gaughan 2005; Harding and Rovit 2005):

- Merger by incorporation, an existing firm incorporates one or more firms;
- Pure merger, two or more firms merge by creating a new legal entity;
- Acquisition, a firm acquires a significant part of the shares of another company.

In an alternative perspective, mergers and acquisitions are categorized with reference to the stimulus to the conclusion of the deal. This stimulus should come from the acquired firm, the purchaser or simultaneously from both firms Bruner 2004a, b; Galpin 2014; Gaughan 2005; Harding and Rovit 2005; Haspeslagh and Jemison 1991).

In the first hypothesis the acquired company "is on sale"; this hypothesis generally come when a firm is distressed and has financial problems, more or less temporary, that impose to acquire new liquidity, not provided by the old property, in order avoiding to compromise business continuity.

In the second case, the input to the conclusion of the deal is grounded in the acquiring company's strategies, so the acquisition is the way to achieve the goals of these strategies.

In the latter case, the acquisition is the result of joint needs or opportunities of both firms with convergent interests to close the transaction.

The acquisitions should be a response to competitors' moves or to anticipate them (Keil et al. 2013). Even companies that do not seem initially oriented to external growth strategies may feel forced to an M&A for fear of becoming themselves "the target of the next deal". Regardless of the reason behind the deal, M&As can be alternatively finalized to the acquisition of a company's control over the other or the birth of a new entity resulting from the merger between the two companies. However, the aim of the deal should be an improvement in the overall performance of the involved firms.

With reference to M&A, the empirical analysis reveals that the worldwide market presented two different growth trend in recent years followed by periods of decline. The period of steady growth during the nineties with an increase of 9 % and 28 % respectively of the number and value of mergers and acquisitions (Bureau Van Dijk 2015) was followed a period of decline experienced between 2001 and 2003. The following shot between the years 2004 and 2007 was followed by a rapid decrease of the operations linked to the economic and financial crisis (Bureau Van Dijk 2015).

The growing importance in the markets led scholars to undertake further research so that the literature has developed several theories to analyze M&A processes (Caiazza and Volpe 2015; Lin 2014; Weber 2013). According to the Internalization Theory (Coase 1937; Williamson 1975), the determinants of M&As are based on synergies or "make or buy" decisions (comparing internal costs and transactional costs market), as well as on the financial logic, induced by the opportunity to invest surplus resources in value-generating activities.

Besides growth size criteria in a hierarchy-market dichotomous view hierarchy-market, prior studies identify additional paradigms related to the concepts of competitive advantage and distinctive resources (Capron et al. 1998), synergistic benefits and synergies (Larsson and Finkelstein 1999), knowledge and cognitive windows. Nowadays, the deal decisions seem increasingly pushed by the presence of underdeveloped resources and knowledge or by the need to monitor markets, products, and sectors behaviours in order to seize the potential opportunities.

Moreover, since M&As generally lead to change processes (Jemison and Sitkin 1986), the literature analyzed organizational issues, such as the impact of the integration needs on organizational changes (Birkinshaw et al. 2000; Cartwright and Cooper 1990; Epstein 2004; Haspeslagh and Farquhar 1994; Marks and Mirvis 2000; Nahavandi and Malekzadeh 1988; Schuler and Jackson 2001; Schweizer and Patzelt 2012; Weber 2011).

Many scholars analysed the critical success and failure factors (Bruner 2004a, b; Hitt et al. 1998). Other empirical analysis investigate the relation between the success of M&A in terms of shareholders value creation, the role of acquisitions experience (Hayward 2002), the stages of deal process (Healy et al. 1992).

Among the quantitative analysis of M&A processes there are numerous researches on performance measurement (Gates and Very 2003; King et al. 2004; Zollo and Meier 2008). The success is usually measured by the rate of return expected by the investor. Prior studies use three main types of measures (Zollo and Meier 2008): weak (increasing share prices); medium (return compared to a benchmark); strong (comparison between the post M&A performance and the expected performance without the deal).

Although success or failure reasons of a deal should be analysed with reference to the features of each M&A, the literature suggest some factors improving the likelihood of success (Barkema and Schijven 2008; Caiazza and Volpe 2015; Cartwright and Schoenberg 2006; Epstein 2005; Hitt et al. 2009; Kpmg 1999; Saint-Onge and Chatzkel 2009; Weber 2013) :

- The complementarity of resources and products of involved companies increases the chances of synergies achievement and the acquisition of a sustainable competitive advantage;
- When the acquisition is "friendly" and is not the result of hostile action of the acquirer firm, the married companies have more opportunities to benefit from the deal by a faster and more efficient integration of the acquired firm;
- From a financial point of view, an acquisition has more possibility to win when the financial leverage is low, since a lower cost of loans will reduce the risk of a dysfunctional deal;
- The acquisition experience and the change management experience of acquiring or acquired firms improve the flexibility and generally favours the integration of corporate cultures;
- An accurate preliminary selection of the acquisition targets is an excellent premise for the post deal performance;
- The emphasis on innovation should be an essential attribute in the current scenarios to sustain a high level of competitiveness of merged firms;
- The attention paid to human resource management can promote acceptance, and collaboration for deal success.

As well as critical success factors, scholars identified some failure reasons such as (Bruner 2002; Gaughan 2005; Hitt et al. 1998; Sirower 1997; Stahl et al. 2013; Vaara 2002):

- The high debt needed for the conclusion of an acquisition undermine the degree of financial leverage resulting in a sensitive negative impact on the performance of the acquiring company;
- Incorrect assessment of the company, or at least approximate acquisition aims, should push to deal failure, since the specific characteristics of the acquired company can be difficult to integrate with the acquiring company;

- Excessive post deal transformations which do not take into due consideration the need for adaptation and integration in the transition period can result in incorrect or inaccurate management of the complex change management process;
- A boost conglomerate diversification, in business far away from the core business, can lead to failure because the acquiring firm has not the skills needed to compete in a new field;
- An excessive number of acquisitions in a too short time horizon should push to lose the focus on critical aspects of each acquisition because the acquiring firm is not able to carefully manage the several change processes.

Despite of studies contribution, most of M&As show results lower than the desired (Capron and Pistre 2002; Capron and Shen 2007; Seyhun 1990; Sirower 1997). M&A results do not generally reflect the ex-ante predictions made for both forecasting mistakes and ineffective management of the integration process (Agarwal and Jaffe 2000; Cormier and Magnan 2005).

There is an increasing attention to the relationship between external strategies, the business combinations and the concept of synergy (Dutordoir et al. 2014). Specifically, there is growing emphasis on the relationships among external strategies and knowledge management, on the one hand, and the synergistic benefits and synergies concepts, on the other.

Research opportunities emerge with regard to synergies, synergies valuation models and synergy achievement. This phenomenon has been the subject of numerous theoretical studies and empirical research but have not yet reached undisputed results on the effective value creation.

Specifically, despite the synergies are considered as one of the critical elements for the success or failure of the deals, the scholars has only partly deepened the issues related to the synergy management. Consequently, the effectiveness of the synergy assessment processes are still heavily discussed in the literature and in the practice.

The relations among strategic management, mergers and acquisitions, and synergy management gain increasing attention.

2.2 The Role of Synergy in Mergers and Acquisitions

M&A is the favorite field study of scholars, even if synergy is sometimes analyzed in the literature independently from M&As (Ex. Friesl and Silberzahn 2012; Goold and Campbell 1998; Garzella 2006; Giannessi 1970; Harrigan 2003; Robins and Wiersema 1995; Strikwerda and Stoelhorst 2009). Moreover, also analysts and managers refer increasingly to the synergy value in most of the relevant M&As in recent years.

Mergers and acquisitions (M&A) deals are a fundamental growth strategy for firms (Collis and Montgomery 1997). Based on the work of Haspeslagh and

Jemison (1991), the M&A process is focused on two main stages: due diligence and integration.

Due diligence is the first stage of the M&A process. A quality pre-acquisition decision-making process, in which the M&A's price and its contribution to the overarching corporate strategy are still under evaluation, is one of the most relevant challenges (Allred et al. 2005; Epstein 2005; Haspeslagh and Jemison 1991; Hitt et al. 1998). Even under conditions of incomplete information, rapidity and secretiveness, firms may avoid "false positive" acquisition opportunities that are generally accepted when they should have been rejected (Evans and Bishop 2001; Zaheer et al. 2013). Consequently, at this stage it is fundamental to consider the risks of a bad synergy valuation (Fiorentino and Garzella 2015; Haspeslagh and Jemison 1991; Rappaport and Sirower 1999). In that respect, the measurement of synergy value is a very relevant issue in M&As and it is not surprising that managers and M&A advisors find the process of synergy assessment to be a challenging task (Garzella and Fiorentino 2014; Slusky and Caves 1991). Conversely, an empirical investigation by Accenture (2007) has shown that synergy expectations are not adequately valorized because typically they are only generally identified and described.

In any event, researchers have shown that what happens at the integration stage is relevant to M&A success (Sales and Mirvis 1984; Buono and Bowditch 1989). Organizational and HRM researchers have noted that potential synergy is not automatically realized and that the extent of synergy realization depends on how the new organization is managed after the "closing date" (Angwin and Urs 2014; Datta 1991; Hunt 1990; Schweiger et al. 1987). Some studies concentrate on how management can achieve potentially synergistic benefits (Birkinshaw et al. 2000; Laarson 1990; Lindgren 1982; Shrivastava 1986). These studies' findings suggest that considerable interaction and coordination are necessary to exploit the synergy that may be present between firms engaged in a merger or acquisition (Haspeslagh and Jemison 1991; Pablo 1994; Shrivastava 1986).

Notwithstanding an intense debate in the literature on this topic (e.g. Bruner 2004a, b; Eccles et al. 1999), theoretical and empirical research still lack a common understanding on the effectiveness of M&A processes (Colombo et al. 2007; Epstein 2005; Gates and Very 2003; Zollo and Meier 2008). Results are often divergent and measurements incomplete (e.g. Bruner 2002). For instance, although there is some evidence on short-term value creation for shareholders in target firms, the empirical support for the creation of long-term value in acquiring firm is still ambiguous (Agarwal and Jaffe 2000; Jensen and Ruback 1983). In addition, despite the advances in M&A researches, scholars show any meaningful difference in M&A failure rate (Cartwright and Schoenberg 2006).

Box 2.1: The Case "AT&T—NCR Corporation"
A typical example of this phenomenon is AT&T's 1991 acquisition of NCR Corporation, one of the largest acquisitions in the computer industry (Lys and Vincent 1995). The acquisition by AT&T resulted in negative synergies of \$1.3–3.0 billion.

The concept of synergy became increasingly diffused in M&As studies and the word "synergy" has enjoyed a very quick diffusion in last years. Synergies were analysed in accounting, finance, management and strategy studies. The idea of synergy was introduced in management literature to explain the additive value created in mergers and acquisitions (Ansoff 1965; Salter and Weinhold 1979; Steiner 1975). From this perspective, scholars defined synergy as "the increase in performance of the combined firm over what the two firms are already expected or required to accomplish as independent firms" (Sirower 1997: 20). However, the concept of synergy is not very clear and it is often characterized by high technical features (Latash 2008).

Over time, the term synergy has started to be used sometimes without any specific definition of the concept and for much more specific meanings (Garzella 2006). For example, in management studies the concept is often related to firm resources: Chatterjee used the term synergy to link value creation and the class of resources (Chatterjee 1986: 120) and Gruca et al. (1997: 605) argued that "the basis for synergy is sharing resources across business activities".

Finance and accounting scholars have instead offered more financially focused alternatives (Leland 2007): Eccles et al. (1999: 140) define synergy as "the net present value of the cash flows that will result from improvements made when the companies are combined"; Slusky and Caves instead present an intermediate approach by linking synergy both to the large premium paid over market value and the relatedness of the businesses of a diversified firm (Slusky and Caves 1991: 277 and 282).

The synergy concept is often used without any definition whilst sometimes there is the definition of some specific type of synergy. The literature review highlights the frequent categorization of synergy by timing. Based on this categorization, scholars discriminate synergy expectations from realized synergy also if in this context there is not sufficient clarity around definitions and notions. Synergy expectations are also called "Potential synergies", and realized synergy are sometimes "Real synergies", other times "Effective synergies" or "Achieved synergies".

Specifically, synergy is relevant in M&A studies about motives, performance such as integration process. Synergy was analyzed in the prior research in the context of both the due-diligence and the integration stage. Studies of due diligence are generally focused on assessment and measurement issues (Colombo et al. 2007), whereas research about integration is primarily based on organizational issues (Vaara 2003). Although the assessment of the value of synergy expectations is regarded as one of the most critical points in M&A performance (Larsson and

Finkelstein 1999), scholars often investigated the causes of differences between the realized and expected synergy value considering the latter as a datum (Bekier and Shelton 2002; Datta and Grant 1990; Gates and Very 2003; Haspeslagh and Jemison 1991; Zollo and Meier 2008). Despite several studies on decision making processes in M&A do exist, those that specifically analyze and assess models of synergy expectation are not many (Chatterjee 1986; Garzella 2006; Gupta and Gerchak 2002; Kode et al. 2003; Damodaran 2005; Rappaport 2006).

This "screwball buzzword" (Lietdka 1998) have produced a paradoxically view of synergy in M&A research. Synergy is simultaneously considered the main reason of value creation and the main reason behind the failures of M&A.

The synergy hypothesis (Seth et al. 2000) is underlying studies about M&A motives. Many scholars lend support to the importance of synergy as a merger motive (Bradley et al. 1988; Kaplan and Weisbac 1992; Sirower 1997; Andrade et al. 2001; Kiymaz and Baker 2008). When synergy is the main motive, these studies conclude that mergers and acquisitions create value for the combined firms and synergy has a positive effect on targets, acquirers and total gains (Berkovitch and Narayanan 1993; Bradley et al. 1988; Sudarsanam et al. 1996).

On the contrary, "synergy inflation" view poses that each M&A initiative embarks on the same enthusiastic quest for synergy achievement (Sirower 1997). This view argues that analysts and managers have overworked the use of the "value of synergy" in most of the relevant M&As that characterized firms and markets growth in recent years. However this diffusion has not always been supported by real synergy achievement in the deals. The findings of prior research show high failure rate of M&As (Bruner 2004a, b; Cartwright and Schoenberg 2006; King et al. 2004; Hitt et al. 2009; Thanos and Papadakis 2012) and scholars underline the role of synergy for explaining this failures (Sirower 1997). Harding and Rovit (2005), building on the results of their research, affirmed that two-thirds of the executives responsible for acquisitions believe to have overestimated the synergic potential and underline the relevance of this error for the deal failure. As in Berkovitch and Narayanan (1993) results, many deals don't create value. As Eccles et al. (1999: 136) emphasise, "many failures occur, though, simply because the acquiring company paid too much for the acquisition".

Overall, scholars and practitioners show that synergy management plays a key role in M&As. Synergy is a relevant motivation of M&A. Where the main motive of M&A is synergy the main risk is synergy inflation. Synergy is not a "trap" per se, but the ineffective management of synergy can drive to synergy pitfalls which could affect the synergy management turning a good M&A in a very bad deal (Hammond et al. 1998). The executives involved in M&A agreements have often underestimated the management of synergy pitfalls and this lack of attention has substantially driven the failures of the deals (Harding and Rovit 2005).

We argue that synergy is not a "myth" and could improve the value of combined firms if managers and executive had able to develop an effective management avoiding hidden pitfalls.

2.3 Synergy: An Important Motivation of M&As

The role of synergy as an important motive in M&As is first analyzed in the strategic management literature by presupposing awareness and comprehension of the fundamental assumptions and key variables of involved firms' growth strategies (Mukherjee et al. 2004).

Box 2.2: The Case "Intesa—San Paolo"
In the M&A report of the deal between the banks Intesa and San Paolo, one of the most relevant mergers in the European bank market, synergy was the main motive of M&A. The integration was expected to generate synergy estimated at approximately € 1550 million per year before taxes, when fully implemented, represented from 63 % of cost savings and the remaining 37 % of additional revenue. As a consequence the net profit was expected to grow at an average annual rate of 14.9 %.

The investigation of synergy as a relevant motive for M&A begins with the resource based view (Barney 1991; Rumelt 1984; Wernefelt 1995) by linking synergy to several classes of resources (Chatterjee 1986) or to the existence of activities in the involved firms' value chains (Porter 1980). Later studies have developed new insights inspired by the theory of dynamic firm capabilities (Nelson 1991; Teece et al. 1997). These contributions have stressed the importance of capabilities exploration and exploitation to create additive performance through strategic alliances and M&As (Arora and Gambardella 1990; Aureli 2015; Eisenhardt and Schoonhoven 1996; Hagedoorn and Duysters 2002; Hitt et al. 1996; Uhlenbruck et al. 2006). A firm's exploitation of existing resources during integration is arguably important for synergy value creation (Barney and Arikan 2001; Sirmon et al. 2007). Another literature stream analyze the synergy motive with reference to the routines of M&A strategies. Idiosyncratic behaviors and organizational path dependencies push firms to concentrate on M&As to realize synergy by reinforcing their existing capabilities (Arikan and McGahan 2010; Harrigan and Newman 1990; Osborn and Hagedoorn 1997; Trautwein 1990).

Despite the strategic management contribution to the "synergy hypothesis", the synergy literature has offered useful, "financially focused" alternatives (Healy et al. 1997; Leland 2007). According to financial logic, firms pursue synergy to reduce their global financial needs and their costs (Jensen and Ruback 1983). The "finance literature" has the merit of highlighting the link between synergy and value creation. To create value, M&A should pursue synergy.

An integrated interpretation of the strategic management and the finance literature suggests that synergy may be the "functional" motive of synergy. When synergy is the primary motive, these studies conclude that mergers and acquisitions can create value for the combined firms and synergy can have a positive effect on targets, acquirers and total gains (Berkovitch and Narayanan 1993; Bradley et al. 1988; Gondhalekar and Bhagwat 2003; Sudarsanam et al. 1996). When no synergy expectations exist, it should be better for firms to pursue internal growth strategies. Synergy may be M&As' "functional" motive because as Zollo and Meier (2008: 60) argue, "if there are no true synergies between the merging firms in the first place, then even to high quality, low-cost implementation of the merger may lead to only negligible benefits".

Box 2.3: The Case "Exxon-Mobil"
Exxon and Mobil, two oil companies, merged in 1998 forming one of the largest companies in the world. This deal, part of an overall consolidation in the oil industry, was first motivated by synergy costs. The aim was to achieve economies of scale without a loss of market share. Since synergy was the M&A functional motive, the deal was successful: cost savings from the merger exceeded the $3.8 billion anticipated synergy by about 20 % (Gaughan 2005).

However, in practice, many M&As are based on additional motives. The literature suggests that executives should put substantial personal motivations before firm motivations (Cartwright and Schoenberg 2006; Nguyen et al. 2012; Seth et al. 2000). The managerialism hypothesis, a key tenet of agency theory, posits that takeovers should be primarily motivated by the self interest of the acquirer's management (Malatesta 1983; Jensen 1986). CEOs may engage in M&As to increase their own power or because managers maximize their own utility at the expense of firm value (Lubatkin 1987; Trautwein 1990). For Black (1989), the interests of executives and managers should diverge from those of their stakeholders. Other times, value destruction acquisitions depend on entrenched managers, who generally choose low-synergy targets and overpay for those synergies (Harford et al. 2012).

Overall, the literature about synergy motives emphasizes relevant insights into synergy management pitfalls. Synergy management may start in pre-deal steps, because it is useful to verify the existence of potential synergy. Moreover, since the sources of potential synergy could be based on either strategy or finances, the synergy assessment should analytically identify several values of synergy. Finally, some synergy pitfalls might hide behind extra-synergy motives.

2.4 Synergy: An Aim Difficult to Realize

Many studies underline the difficulties in realizing expected synergy. These studies generally focus on the likelihood of realizing synergy with reference to the features of both of the firms involved, along with the types of M&As involved.

Studies inspired by the resource based theory and the theory of firm dynamic capabilities suggest that there is an association among firm-level factors, industry, geographic context and synergy realization (Oster 1992; Roberts and Berry 1985; Hagedoorn and Duysters 2002). For example, some scholars (e.g., Bradley et al. 1988) have suggested that deal failure is negatively correlated to the degree of relatedness of the involved firms; however, others have found that the likelihood of failure is greater in related mergers (Lubatkin 1987; Harrison et al. 1991). Studies have also analyzed the likelihood of achieving different types of synergies with reference to deal features such as horizontal/non-horizontal, related/unrelated or complementary/similar (Chatterjee 1986; Makri et al. 2010; Zaheer et al. 2013). Another less-explored area argues that the achievement of synergy is made difficult by causal ambiguity (Lippman and Rumelt 1982) resulting from a lack of understanding.

Box 2.4: The Case "AOL—Time Warner"
AOL announced the Time Warner acquisition for $165 billion in January 2000. Before the merger, AOL originally was a dial up providing service firm. Time Warner, formed in 1990 through the merger of Time Inc. and Warner Communications, was a firm operating in media and entertainment.

In the M&A between AOL and Time Warner the potential synergies, by distributing Time Warner's films and music over AOL's global internet network, were never realized (Gaughan 2005; Klein 2003).

Indeed, strategic management scholars suggest that synergy achievement becomes increasingly difficult over time (Haspeslagh and Jemison 1991; Hintherhuber 2002). On the one hand, the temporal lag between closing and the beginning of integration "has the strongest and most negative effect on the acquisition performance" (Colombo et al. 2007: 215). On the other hand, integration speed can positively or negatively influence the success of an M&A deal (Homburg and Bucerius 2006). Firms should effectively choose between lower short-term and higher long-term synergy.

The easy of realization of synergy has also been analyzed in the context of "learning by doing" processes (Nelson and Winter 1982). The processes of due diligence, negotiation and integration are dynamic (Shimuzu et al. 2004). The M&A experience reduces the difficulties of synergy realization because M&A makes not only the acquisition and the assessment of synergy information but also the exploitation of M&A opportunities more efficient (Collins et al. 2009; Finkelstein and Haleblian 2002; Hayward 2002; Hitt et al. 2001).

Another substantive body of research has been developed by organizational and human resource management scholars. This field of inquiry is directed at the cultural dynamics of M&A. This literature has sought to analyze the impact of variables such as "cultural distance", "cultural compatibility", and "cultural change" on M&A performance (Cartwright and Cooper 1996; Morosini et al. 1998; Kavanagh and Ashkanasy 2006; Stahl and Voight 2008). These studies suggest that cultural differences can create major obstacles to synergy achievement (Stahl and Voight 2008). A well-designed integration process is critical to capture all forecasted synergies (Birkinshaw et al. 2000). Specifically, socio-cultural integration and task integration results are critical for synergy realization (Stahl and Voight 2008). The challenge is to select a set of tools that are realizable within the firms' capacities to cope with changes and to absorb resource constraints (Kavanagh and Ashkanasy 2006).

Financial studies argues that if all other conditions are equal, the value of synergies is negatively correlated to the timing of their realization (Copeland 1994; Rappaport 1986). This issue represents a relevant decisional problem in M&A and makes the likelihood of synergy achievement a relevant factor for synergy management (Cullinan et al. 2004; Damodaran 2005; Evans and Bishop 2001).

Moreover, on the practitioners' side, surveys conducted by advisors and consultants—which have demonstrated difficulties in realizing synergy—show that revenue growth and cost-saving synergies have different levels of achievement (Accenture 2007; KPMG 1999). Specifically, the likelihood of success of each type of synergy depends on both the difficulty of assessment and the intensity of implementation efforts (Garzella and Fiorentino 2014).

In short, this second area of investigation provides additional insights about the pitfalls of synergy management. Because the achievement of expected synergies is generally difficult, in the pre-deal steps firms should estimate the difficulties and the integration costs. Moreover, the integration approach, according to the analysis of potential synergy and organizational difficulties, should be developed prior to concluding the deal.

Box 2.5: The Case "Accenture HR Services—TE.SS (Telecom Italia Group)"

In 2002, TE.SS Spa, the human resource management company of Telecom Italian Group, was acquired by Accenture, becoming part, from March 2003, of Accenture HR Services, the Accenture Group company dedicated to human resource management services.

The integration of TE.SS. and Accenture HR Services was not granted. However, in the due-diligence stage Accenture carefully analyzed the possible difficulties in the process of integration since the know-how and knowledge of TE.SS was very different from Accenture methodologies and management processes. The operation was potentially dangerous because of the comparison and synthesis effort between two cultures and two business models inspired by different logics. TE.SS had a "role culture" whilst Accenture HR Services had a "task culture" (Cartwright and Cooper 1996).

(continued)

Box 2.5 (continued)

This case, however, pointed out that the ability to assess potential problems can help develop the critical skills necessary to face the integration process between involved companies.

In addition, the case has highlighted the centrality of the possible integration costs and risks. The early prediction of risks has achieved a good acceptance of change and a great level of integration between the cultural roots of two different groups, Telecom Italia and Accenture (Fiorentino 2013).

The difficulties estimated may involve many of the issues highlighted in the various literature streams. Furthermore, the distinction between revenue growth and cost-saving synergies should be useful in the assessment process to identify potential difficulties at the integration stage. These issues imply adding organization fit to the strategic fit analysis. Consequently, the literature suggests the importance of the integration step. Finally, some other pitfalls should be derived derive from a lack of attention to organizational issues.

2.5 Synergy: The Risks

Many scholars, primarily in the strategic and finance literature, analyze the degree of synergy realization in M&A. These studies often argue that although each M&A initiative embarks on the same enthusiastic quest for synergy achievement, synergy is generally unrealized in most M&As: synergies are often promised but seldom realized (Sirower 1997). As in Berkovitch and Narayanan's (1993) results, many deals do not create value.

Box 2.6: The Case "Daimler Benz—Chrysler"

In 1998, German-based Daimler Benz and US-based Chrysler merged in one of the most relevant deals in the automotive industry. The two firms were profitable before the merger. Daimler Benz, was searching for a US acquisition in its globalization strategy. Chrysler appeared to have the highest synergistic potential: it was strong in the geographical markets where Daimler was weaker. However, after the merger Daimler's profitability fall down and Chrysler begin to obtain record losses. The mergers was a failure and the most of the expected synergy was never realized (Bower 2001; Neubauer et al. 2000).

The identification of synergy trap pushes studies to measure the magnitude of the trap and to analyze its causes and potential solutions.

Most of the strategic management, organizational behavior and change management literature about "the synergy trap" was focused on explaining the motives for and performance of poor deal management. An incomplete list of the reasons that a deal might be at risk includes the following: complexity, secrecy, speed, distortive informative processes, inappropriate managerial backgrounds, agreements with professional firms, high levels of competition, ineffective assessment models, economic disturbances, hubris, overconfidence, high control costs, high coordination costs, self interest on the part of the acquirer's management, the absence of plans to deliver synergies, the absence of sole responsibility in synergy deliverance, retention of top management, poor HR relevance, change inertia, and cultural differences (Doz and Hamel 1998; Kiymaz and Baker 2008; Sparks 1998).

According to "attention based view" studies (Occasio 1997; Simon 1947), one cause of M&A failure is the bounded individual rationality that results from limited attention capacity and incomplete knowledge of both action alternatives and action effects (Jeris et al. 2002; Shield et al. 2002; Yu et al. 2005). The arguments made by these studies argue that because the due-diligence and integration stages absorb significant amounts of energy and attention, executives' attention should be diverted from core actions (Ghemawat and Ghadar 2000; Hitt et al. 1998; Vaara 2003). As a consequence, the lack of attention should sometimes affect synergy measurement at the pre-deal stages and other times should affect issues related to synergy achievement and integration (Greenwood et al. 2004).

The agency theory posits the existence of agency conflicts among several stakeholders involved in M&As. Scholars underline the conflicts related to managers, investment banks, and professional firms. Management, or part of it, often follows distorted information processes that attempt to pursue objectives that do not fit (either completely or partially) with the firms' aims (Haspeslagh and Jemison 1991; Kpmg 1999; Simon 1964). When the self-interest of the acquirer's management comes before the firm's interests, there is the risk that difficulties will be underestimated (Malatesta 1983; Jensen 1986). Conflicts may also be related to investment banks involved in the advising and closings stages of M&As (Angwin 2001; Haunschild and Miner 1997). Information asymmetries with other professional firms (consultants, law firms, independent auditors) may cause a push to pay premiums that are too high (Porter 1987; Shimuzu et al. 2004). Agency costs resulting from management decisions imply greater difficulties in transforming potential synergy into achieved synergy (Mueller and Sirower 2003).

As Gort's (1969) theory suggests, synergy assessment could be affected by economic disturbances that cause changes in individual expectations and increase uncertainty.

Indeed, the existence of several acquiring companies that compete to secure a deal pushes top management to overestimate synergy. Furthermore, management with inappropriate backgrounds and inappropriate agreements with advisors may result in poor synergy valuation (Fiorentino and Garzella 2014).

The RBV posits that causal ambiguity between integration decisions and M&A performance outcomes should be a key determinant of deal failure (Cording et al. 2008). This causal ambiguity refers to a lack of understanding between a firm's resources and synergy outcomes. Interfirm and intrafirm causal ambiguity coexist (King 2007). At the due-diligence stage, when firms seeks to reduce ambiguity by gaining access to the detailed information that enables synergy assessment, interfirm causal ambiguity is present (Pablo 1994). At the integration stage, interfirm causal ambiguity shifts to intrafirm causal ambiguity when managers do not understand how their decisions affect synergy realization. Ambiguity limits executives' capacity to predict the outcome of synergy implementation decisions, thus leading to suboptimal decisions (King and Zeithaml 2001). M&A failures occur after inappropriate decisions and integration processes that lead to realized synergy inferior to what was expected.

The hubris and the market efficiency theories argue that M&As are related to CEOs' hubris or overconfidence (Hayward and Hambrick 1997; Roll 1986). The hubris hypothesis posits that firms engage in acquisitions even when no synergy exists. Top management make systematic mistakes in evaluating synergies and the takeover premium merely reflects a random error. Consequently, takeovers occur only because acquirers make mistakes in estimating gains (Berkovitch and Narayanan 1993). According to this hubris-based view, managerial over-optimism systematically leads to overly optimistic synergy expectations. This happens even if the strong-form assumption of the hubris hypothesis by the market efficiency theory rejects any synergy hypothesis.

The financial studies, which are primarily based on event studies, arrive at additional results (Agarwal and Jaffe 2000). The risk of "synergy trap" is generally linked to the premium over the price paid to acquire potential synergies. Indeed, starting from the synergy trap, finance scholars have investigated the failure to achieve synergy with respect to the source of value destruction (Harford et al. 2012).

Other studies focus on the examination of how the synergy trap can be either avoided or limited. Scholars have suggested tools, behaviors and actions to overcame the risks of unsuccessful synergy achievement. A nonexhaustive list of suggested practical solutions includes the following: pay careful attention to the advisory agreement; verify the alignment between one's strategy and the deal; pay attention to the action plan; conduct a careful analysis of the reasons to engage in M&A activity; to give more relevance to the audit committee; to carefully organize the relationships among managers of different companies; to establish a termination fee; to build cross-functional teams from technical, operational and financial positions; to take a risk-management approach to board-level discussion; and to assess carefully the "synergy value" (e.g. Cullinan et al. 2004; Gomes et al. 2013; Hitt et al. 2009).

Therefore, this literature stream suggests the relevance of synergy pitfalls. The existence of several causes implies the existence of multiple types of risk. However, studies reattach the risks of an unsuccessful synergy achievement to a single "trap", whereas research that examines the several types of pitfalls that may hinder the success of M&A deals, and the mistakes related to synergy assessment and realization remain surprisingly limited (Fiorentino and Garzella 2015; Goold and Campbell 1998; Hitt et al. 2009).

Because risks are reattached to a single and generic trap, managers and advisors have been given little guidance on the specific causes of "synergy pitfalls" and on the most effective way to avoid them. Consequently, this gap requires the careful identification of the main types of synergy pitfalls by connecting to each pitfall the related cause and the most useful solutions.

The integrative analysis of the three broad areas of investigation of synergy management suggests relevant insights about synergy management. Overall, the ineffective management of synergy is a relevant risk in M&As. There are many pitfalls, and not a single trap, that could affect the synergy management that transforms a good M&A into a very bad deal (Fiorentino and Garzella 2015; Hammond et al. 1998). The executives involved in M&A agreements have often underestimated the management of synergy pitfalls, and this lack of attention has substantially driven deal failure (Harding and Rovit 2005). Despite significant progress, the extant synergy management literature still suffers from several shortcomings. There is a lack of integration across research paths pertinent to the study of synergy management.

We contribute to the existing literature by improving the analysis in the strategic management literature, considering and incorporating insights from new streams and the contiguous literature. Indeed, we answer to the call for further research about "how" to manage synergy pitfalls by developing a comprehensive framework that is useful for both scholars and practitioners.

References

Aaker DA (2008) Strategic market management. Wiley, New York, NY

Abell DF (1980) Defining the business. The starting point of strategic planning. Prentice-Hall, Englewood Cliffs, NJ

Accenture (2007) Strategy in action. The synergy enigma. http://www.accenture.com

Agarwal A, Jaffe JF (2000) The post-merger performance puzzle. In: Cooper C, Gregory A (eds) Advances in mergers and acquisitions, vol 1. Elsevier Science, New York, NY, pp 7–14

Alexander M (1997) Managing the boundaries of the organization. Long Range Plan 30 (5):787–789

Allred BB, Boal KB, Holstein WK (2005) Corporations as stepfamilies: a new metaphor for explaining the fate of merged and acquired companies. Acad Manag Exec 19(3):23–37

Andrade GM, Mitchell ML, Stafford E (2001) New evidence and perspectives on mergers. Harvard Business School Working paper, No. 01-070. http://ssrn.com/abstract=269313

Andrews KR (1971) The concept of corporate strategy. Dow Jones Irwin, Homewood, IL

Angwin DN (2001) Mergers and acquisitions across European borders: national perspectives on pre-acquisition due diligence and the use of professional advisors. J World Bus 36(1):32–57

Angwin DN, Urs U (2014) The effect of routine amalgamations in post-acquisition integration performance: whether to 'Combine' or 'Superimpose' for synergy gains? Adv Mergers Acquis 13:153–179

Ansoff HI (1965) Corporate strategy. McGraw-Hill, New York, NY

Arikan AM, McGahan AM (2010) The development of capabilities in new firms. Strateg Manag J 31(1):1–18
Arora A, Gambardella A (1990) Complementary and external linkages: the strategies of large firms in biotechnology. J Ind Econ 38(4):361–379
Aureli S (2015) Performance of unlisted Italian companies acquired by multinationals from emerging markets: the case of Indian acquisitions. J Organ Chang Manag 28(5):895–924
Barkema HG, Schijven M (2008) Toward unlocking the full potential of acquisitions. Acad Manag J 51(4):696–722
Barney JB (1991) Firms resources and sustained competitive advantage. J Manag 17(1):99–120
Barney JB (1999) How firm capabilities affect boundary decisions. Sloan Manag Rev 40(1):19–32
Barney J, Arikan A (2001) The resource-based view: origins and implications. In: Hitt MA, Freeman E, Harrison J (eds) The Blackwell handbook of strategic management. Blackwell Business, Oxford, pp 124–188
Bekier MM, Shelton MJ (2002) Keeping your sales force after the merger. McKinsey Q 12 (4):106–115
Berkovitch E, Narayanan MP (1993) Motives for takeovers: an empirical investigation. J Financ Quant Anal 28(3):347–362
Bertini U (1990) Il sistema d'azienda. Schema di analisi. Giappichelli, Torino
Bertini U (1995) Scritti di politica aziendale. Giappichelli, Torino
Bianchi Martini S (2009) Introduzione all'analisi strategica dell'azienda. Giappichelli, Torino
Birkinshaw J, Bresman H, Håkanson L (2000) Managing the post-acquisition integration process: how the human integration and task integration processes interact to foster value creation. J Manag Stud 37(3):395–425
Black BS (1989) Bidder overpayments in takeovers. Stanford Law Rev 41:597–653
Boulding KE (1981) General systems theory—the skeleton of science. In: AA,VV (eds) Management classic. Goodyear Publishing, Culver City, CA
Bower J (2001) Not all M&A's are alike—and that matters. Harv Bus Rev 79(3):92–101
Bradley M, Desai A, Kim HE (1988) Synergistic gains from corporate acquisitions and their divisions between the stockholders of target and acquiring firms. J Financ Econ 21(1):3–40
Bruner RF (2002) Does M&A pay? A survey of evidence for the decision maker. J Appl Financ Theory Pract Educ 12(1):48–88
Bruner RF (2004a) Applied mergers and acquisitions. Wiley, New York, NY, p 173
Bruner RF (2004b) Deals from hell: M&A Lessons that rise above the ashes. Wiley, New York, NY
Buono AF, Bowditch JL (1989) The human side of mergers and acquisitions. Jossey-Bass, San Francisco, CA
Bureau Van Dijk (2015) Zephyr annual M&A report 2014, BV DEP 2015
Caiazza R, Volpe T (2015) M&A process: a literature review and research agenda. Bus Process Manag J 21(1):205–220
Capron L, Pistre N (2002) When do acquirers earn abnormal returns? Strateg Manag J 23 (9):781–794
Capron L, Shen J (2007) Acquisition of private vs. public firms: private information, target selection, and acquirer returns. Strateg Manag J 28(9):891–911
Capron L, Dussuage P, Mitchell W (1998) Resource redeployment following horizontal acquisitions in Europe and North America, 1988–92. Strateg Manag J 19(7):631–661
Cartwright S, Cooper CL (1990) The impact of mergers and acquisitions on people at work: existing research and issues. Br J Manag 1(2):65–76
Cartwright S, Cooper CL (1996) Managing mergers, acquisitions, and strategic alliances: integrating people and cultures. Butterworth-Heinemann, Oxford
Cartwright S, Schoenberg R (2006) Thirty years of mergers and acquisitions research: recent advances and future opportunities. Br J Manag 17(S1):s1–s5
Chatterjee S (1986) Types of synergy and economic value: the impact of acquisitions on merging and rival firms. Strateg Manag J 7(2):119–139

Coase RH (1937) The nature of the firm. Economica 4(16):386–405
Collins JD, Holcomb TR, Trevis Certo S, Hitt MA, Lester RH (2009) Learning by doing: cross-border mergers and acquisitions. J Bus Res 62(12):1329–1334
Collis DJ, Montgomery CA (1997) Corporate strategy. McGraw-Hill, New York, NY
Colombo G, Conca V, Buongiorno M, Gnan L (2007) Integrating cross-border acquisitions: a process-oriented approach. Long Range Plan 40(2):202–222
Copeland T (1994) Why value value? McKinsey Q 4:97–109
Cording M, Christmann P, King DR (2008) Reducing causal ambiguity in acquisition integration: intermediate goals as mediators of integration decisions and acquisition performance. Acad Manag J 51(4):744–767
Cormier D, Magnan ML (2005) From accounting to "Forecounting". Can Account Perspect 4 (2):243–255
Cullinan G, Le Roux J, Weddigen R (2004) When to walk away from a deal. Harv Bus Rev 82 (4):96–105
Cummings JL, Holmberg SR (2012) Best-fit alliance partners: the use of critical success factors in a comprehensive partner selection process. Long Range Plan 45(2–3):136–159
Damodaran A (2005) The value of Synergy. Stern School of Business, New York, NY. Available at SSRN 841486(2005). October 30, 2005
Datta DK (1991) Organizational fit and acquisition performance: effects of post-acquisition integration. Strateg Manag J 12(4):281–297
Datta DK, Grant JH (1990) Relationships between type of acquisition, the autonomy given to the acquired firm, and acquisition success: an empirical analysis. J Manag 16(2):29–44
Doz YL, Hamel G (1998) Alliance advantage: the art of creating value through partnering. Harvard Business School Press, Boston, MA
Dutordoir M, Roosenboom P, Vasconcelos M (2014) Synergy disclosures in mergers and acquisitions. Int Rev Financ Anal 31(1):88–100
Dyer JH, Singh H (1998) The relational view: cooperative strategy and sources of interorganizational competitive advantage. Acad Manag Rev 23(4):660–679
Eccles RG, Lanes KL, Wilson TC (1999) Are you paying too much for that acquisition? Harv Bus Rev 77(4):136–146
Eisenhardt KM, Schoonhoven CB (1996) Resource-based view of strategic alliance formation: strategic and social effects in entrepreneurial firms. Organ Sci 7(2):136–150
Epstein MJ (2004) The drivers of success in post merger integration. Organ Dyn 33(2):174–189
Epstein MJ (2005) The determinants and evaluation of merger success. Bus Horiz 48(5):37–46
Evans FC, Bishop DM (2001) Valuation for M&A: building value in private companies. Wiley, New York, NY
Finkelstein S, Haleblian J (2002) Understanding acquisition performance: the role of transfer effects. Organ Sci 13(1):36–47
Fiorentino R (2013) Il change management nei processi d'integrazione tra aziende. Aracne Editrice, Roma
Fiorentino R, Garzella S (2014) The synergy valuation models: towards the real value of mergers and acquisitions. Int Res J Financ Econ 124:71–82
Fiorentino R, Garzella S (2015) Synergy pitfalls management in mergers and acquisitions. Manag Decis 53(7):1469–1501
Foss NJ (1996) Knowledge-based approaches to the theory of the firm: some critical comments. Organ Sci 7(5):470–476
Freeman RE (1984) Strategic management. A stakeholder approach. Pitman, New York, NY
Friesl M, Silberzahn R (2012) Challenges in establishing global collaboration. Long Range Plan 45(2–3):160–181
Galeotti M, Garzella S (2013) Governo strategico dell'azienda. Giappichelli, Torino
Galpin TJ (2014) The complete guide to mergers and acquisitions: process tools to support M&A integration at every level. Wiley, New York, NY
Garzella S (2000) I confini dell'azienda. Giuffré, Milano

Garzella S (2006) Il governo delle sinergie. Giappichelli, Torino
Garzella S, Fiorentino R (2014) A synergy measurement model to support the pre-deal decision making in mergers and acquisitions. Manag Decis 52(6):1194–1216
Gates S, Very P (2003) Measuring performance during M&A integration. Long Range Plan 36 (2):167–186
Gaughan PA (2005) Mergers: what can go wrong and how to prevent it. Wiley, New York, NY
Ghemawat P, Ghadar F (2000) The dubious logic of global megamergers. Harv Bus Rev 78 (4):65–72
Giannessi E (1970) Appunti di economia aziendale. Pacini, Pisa
Gomes E, Angwin DN, Weber Y, Tarba SY (2013) Critical success factors through the mergers and acquisitions process: revealing pre- and post-M&A connections for improved performance. Thunderbird Int Bus Rev 55(1):13–35
Gondhalekar V, Bhagwat Y (2003) Motives in the acquisitions of NASDAQ targets during the aftermath of the 1987 crash. Financ Rev 38(4):553–569
Goold M, Campbell A (1998) Desperately seeking synergy. Harv Bus Rev 76:131–143
Gort M (1969) An economic disturbance theory of mergers. Q J Econ 83(4):624–642
Grant RM (2015) Contemporary strategy analysis 9e text only. Wiley, New York, NY
Greenwood R, Hinnings CR, Brown J (2004) Momentum and serendipity: how acquired leaders create value in the integration of technology firms. Strateg Manag J 25(8–9):751–777
Gruca TS, Nath D, Mehra A (1997) Exploiting synergy for competitive advantage. Long Range Plan 30(4):605–611
Gupta D, Gerchak Y (2002) Quantifying operational synergies in a merger/acquisition. Manag Sci 18:517–533
Guth WD (1980) Corporate growth strategies. J Bus Strateg 1(2):56–62
Hagedoorn J, Duysters G (2002) External sources of innovative capabilities: the preference for strategic alliances or mergers and acquisitions. J Manag Stud 39(2):167–188
Hamel G, Prahalad CK (2013) Competing for the future. Harvard Business Press, Boston, MA
Hammond JS, Keeney RL, Raiffa H (1998) The hidden traps in decision making. Harv Bus Rev 76 (5):47–58
Harding D, Rovit S (2005) Mastering the merger: four critical decisions that make or break the deal. Harvard Business School Press, Boston, MA
Harford J, Humphery-Jenner M, Powell R (2012) The sources of value destruction in acquisitions by entrenched managers. J Financ Econ 106(2):247–261
Hargadon A (2002) Brokering knowledge: linking learning and innovation. In: Staw BM, Kramer RM (eds) Research in organizational behavior, vol 24. JAI Press, Greenwich, CT, pp 41–85
Harrigan K (2003) Joint ventures, alliances, and corporate strategy. Beard Books, Washington, DC
Harrigan KR, Newman WH (1990) Bases of interorganization co-operation: propensity, power, persistence. J Manag Stud 27(4):417–434
Harrison JS, Hitt MA, Hoskisson RE, Ireland RD (1991) Synergies and post-acquisition performance: differences versus similarities in resource allocations. J Manag 17(1):173–190
Haspeslagh P, Farquhar AB (1994) The acquisition integration process: a contingent framework. In: Von Krogh G, Siknatra A, Singh H (eds) The management of corporate acquisitions. Macmillan, London
Haspeslagh PC, Jemison DB (1991) Managing acquisitions. Free Press, New York, NY
Haunschild PR, Miner AS (1997) Modes of interorganizational imitation: the effects of outcome salience and uncertainty. Adm Sci Q 42(3):472–500
Hayward MLA (2002) When do firms learn from their acquisition experience? Evidence from 1990-1995. Strateg Manag J 23(1):21–39
Hayward MLA, Hambrick DC (1997) Explaining the premiums paid for large acquisitions: evidence of CEO hubris. Admin Sci Q 42(1):103–127
Healy PM, Palepu KG, Ruback RS (1992) Does corporate performance improve after mergers? J Financ Econ 31(2):135–175

Healy PM, Palepu KG, Ruback RS (1997) Which takeovers are profitable? Strategic or financial? Sloan Manag Rev 38(4):45–57

Hill C, Gareth J, Schilling M (2014) Strategic management: theory: an integrated approach. Cengage Learning, Mason, OH

Hintherhuber HH (2002) Taking time to integrate temporal research. Acad Manag Rev 27(2):170

Hitt MA, Hoskisson RE, Johnson RA, Moesel DD (1996) The market for corporate control and firm innovation. Acad Manag J 39(5):1084–1119

Hitt M, Harrison J, Ireland RD, Best A (1998) Attributes of successful and unsuccessful acquisitions of US firms. Br J Manag 9(2):91–114

Hitt MA, Dacin MT, Levitas E, Arregle JL, Borza A (2000) Partner selection in emerging and developed market contexts: resource-based and organizational learning perspectives. Acad Manag J 43(3):449–467

Hitt MA, Harrison JS, Ireland RD (2001) Mergers and acquisitions: a guide to creating value for stakeholders. Oxford University Press, New York, NY

Hitt M, King D, Kriishnan H, Makri M, Schijven K, Zhu H (2009) Mergers and acquisitions: overcoming pitfalls, building synergy, and creating value. Bus Horiz 52(6):523–529

Holcomb TR, Hitt MA (2007) Toward a model of strategic outsourcing. J Oper Manag 25 (2):464–481

Homburg C, Bucerius M (2006) Is speed of integration really a success factor of mergers and acquisitions? An analysis of the role of internal and external relatedness. Strateg Manag J 27 (4):347–367

Hunt JW (1990) Changing pattern of acquisition behaviour in takeovers and the consequences for acquisition processes. Strateg Manag J 11(1):69–77

Jemison DB, Sitkin SB (1986) Corporate acquisitions: a process perspective. Acad Manag Rev 11 (1):145–163

Jensen MC (1986) Agency costs of free cash flow, corporate finance, and takeovers. Am Econ Rev 76(2):323–329

Jensen MC, Ruback RS (1983) The market for corporate control: the scientific evidence. J Financ Econ 11(1–4):5–50

Jeris LS, Johnson RJ, Anthony CC (2002) HRD involvement in merger and acquisition decisions and strategy development: four organizational portrait. Int J Train Dev 6(1):2–12

Kaplan S, Weisbac MS (1992) The success of acquisitions: evidence from divestitures. J Financ 47 (1):107–138

Kavanagh MH, Ashkanasy NM (2006) The impact of leadership and change management strategy on organizational culture and individual acceptance of change during a merger. Br J Manag 17 (s1):S81–S103

Keil T, Laamanen T, McGrath RG (2013) Is a counterattack the best defense? Competitive dynamics through acquisitions. Long Range Plan 46(3):195–215

King AW (2007) Disentangling interfirm and intrafirm causal ambiguity: a conceptual model of causal ambiguity and sustainable competitive advantage. Acad Manag Rev 32(1):156–178

King AW, Zeithaml CP (2001) Competencies and firm performance: examining the causal ambiguity paradox. Strateg Manag J 22(1):75–99

King DR, Dalton DR, Daily CD, Covin JG (2004) Meta-analyses of post-acquisition performance: indications of unidentified moderators. Strateg Manag J 25(2):187–200

Kiymaz H, Baker HK (2008) Short-term performance, industry effects, and motives: evidence from large M&As. Q J Financ Account 47(2):17–44

Klein A (2003) Stealing time: Steve Case, Jerry Levin, and the collapse of AOL Time Warner. Simon & Schuster, New York, NY

Kode GVM, Ford JC, Sutherland MM (2003) A conceptual model for evaluation of synergies in mergers and acquisitions. South Afr J Bus 48(1):27–38

KPMG (1999) Unlocking shareholder value: the keys to success. KPMG, London

Laarson R (1990) Coordination of action in mergers and acquisitions. Interpretative and system approaches towards synergy. Lund University Press, Lund, Sweden

Larsson R, Finkelstein S (1999) Integrating strategic, organizational, and human resource perspectives on mergers and acquisitions: a case survey of synergy realization. Organ Sci 10 (1):1–26
Latash ML (2008) Synergy. Oxford University Press, New York, NY
Leland HE (2007) Financial synergies and the optimal scope of the firm: implications for mergers, spinoffs, and structured finance. J Financ 62(2):765–807
Lietdka JM (1998) Synergy revisited: how a "Screwball Buzzword" can be good for the bottom line. Bus Strateg Rev 9(2):45–55
Lin LH (2014) Organizational structure and acculturation in acquisitions perspectives of congruence theory and task interdependence. J Manag 40(7):1831–1856
Lindgren U (1982) Foreign acquisition management of the integration process. IIB/EFI, Stockholm, Sweden
Lippman S, Rumelt R (1982) uncertain imitability: an analysis of interfirm differences in efficiency under competition. Bell J Econ 13(2):418–438
Lubatkin M (1987) Merger strategies and stockholder value. Strateg Manag J 8(1):39–53
Luhmann N (1995) Social systems. Stanford University Press, Stanford, CA
Lys T, Vincent L (1995) An analysis of the value destruction in AT&T's acquisition of NCR. J Financ Econ 39(2):353–378
Makri M, Hitt M, Lane PJ (2010) Complementary technologies, knowledge relatedness, and invention outcomes in high technology mergers and acquisitions. Strateg Manag J 31:602–628
Malatesta PH (1983) The wealth effect of merger activity and the objective functions of merging firms. J Financ Econ 11(1–4):155–181
Marks ML, Mirvis PH (2000) Managing mergers, acquisitions, and alliances: creating an effective transition structure. Organ Dyn 28(3):35–47
McEvily B, Zaheer A (1999) Bridging ties: a source of firm heterogeneity in competitive capabilities. Strateg Manag J 20(12):1133–1156
Mintzberg H, Ahlstrand B, Lampel J (2005) Strategy safari. Simon & Schuster, New York, NY
Morosini P, Shane S, Singh H (1998) National cultural distance and cross-border acquisition performance. J Int Bus Stud 29:137–158
Mueller DC, Sirower ML (2003) The causes of mergers: tests based on the gains to acquiring firms' shareholders and the size of premia. Manag Decis Econ 24(5):373–391
Mukherjee TK, Kiymaz H, Baker K (2004) Merger motives and target valuation: a survey of evidence from CFOs. J Appl Financ 14(2):7–24
Nahavandi A, Malekzadeh AR (1988) Acculturation in mergers and acquisitions. Acad Manag Rev 13(1):79–90
Nelson R (1991) Why do firms differ, and how does it matter? Strateg Manag J 12:61–74
Nelson R, Winter S (1982) An evolutionary theory of economic change. Belknap, Cambridge, MA
Neubauer F, Steger U, Rädler G (2000) The Daimler/Chrysler merger: the involvement of the boards. Corp Gov Int Rev 8(4):375–387
Nguyen HT, Yung K, Sun Q (2012) Motives for mergers and acquisitions: *ex-post* market evidence from the US. J Bus Financ Account 39(9–10):1357–1375
Normann R (1977) Managing for growth. Wiley, New York, NY
Occasio W (1997) Towards an attention-based view of the firm. Strateg Manag J 18:187–206
Osborn RN, Hagedoorn J (1997) The institutionalization and evolutionary dynamics of interorganizational alliances and networks. Acad Manag J 40:261–278
Oster SM (1992) Modern competitive analysis. Oxford University Press, New York, NY
Pablo A (1994) Determinants of acquisition integration level: a decision-making perspective. Acad Manag J 37(4):803–836
Parmigiani A, Mitchell W (2009) Complementarity, capabilities, and the boundaries of the firm: the impact of within-firm and interfirm expertise on concurrent sourcing of complementarity components. Strateg Manag J 30(10):1065–1091
Porter ME (1980) Competitive strategy. Free Press, New York, NY
Porter ME (1987) From competitive advantage to corporate strategy. Harv Bus Rev 65(3):43–59

Porter ME (2008) Competitive strategy: techniques for analyzing industries and competitors. Simon and Schuster, New York, NY

Rappaport A (1986) Creating shareholder value: the new standard for business performance. Free Press, New York, NY

Rappaport A (2006) Ten ways to create shareholder value. Harv Bus Rev 88(9):66–77

Rappaport A, Sirower ML (1999) Stock or cash? The trade-offs for buyers and sellers in mergers and acquisitions. Harv Bus Rev 77(6):147–158

Roberts ER, Berry CA (1985) Entering new businesses: selecting strategies for success. Sloan Manag Rev 26:3–17

Robins J, Wiersema MF (1995) A resource based approach to the multibusiness firm: empirical analysis of portfolio interrelationship and corporate financial performance. Strateg Manag J 16 (4):277–299

Roll R (1986) The Hubris hypothesis of corporate takeovers. J Bus 59:197–216

Rothaermel FT (2015) Strategic management. McGraw-Hill, New York, NY

Rumelt RP (1984) Toward a strategic theory of the firm. In: Lamb R (ed) Competitive strategic management. Prentice Hall, Englewood Cliffs, NJ, pp 556–570

Saint-Onge H, Chatzkel J (2009) Beyond the deal: a revolutionary framework for successful mergers & acquisitions that achieve breakthrough performance gains. McGraw-Hill, New York, NY

Sales AL, Mirvis PH (1984) When cultures collide: issue in acquisitions. In: Kimberley J, Quinn R (eds) New futures: the challenge of managing corporate transitions. Dow-Jones, Irwin, Homewood

Salter M, Weinhold WA (1979) Diversification through acquisition: strategies for creating economic value. Free Press, New York, NY

Santos FA, Eisenhardt KA (2005) Organizational boundaries and theories of organization. Organ Sci 16(5):491–508

Schuler R, Jackson S (2001) HR issues and activities in mergers and acquisitions. Eur Manag J 19 (3):239–253

Schweiger DM, Ivancevich JM, Frank R (1987) Power executive actions for managing human resources before and after acquisition. Acad Manag Exec 1(2):127–138

Schweizer L, Patzelt H (2012) Employee commitment in the post-acquisition integration process: the effect of integration speed and leadership. Scand J Manag 28(4):298–310

Seth A, Song KP, Richardson Pettit R (2000) Synergy, managerialism or Hubris? An empirical examination of motives for foreign acquisitions of U.S. firms. J Bus Stud 31(3):387–405

Seyhun HN (1990) Do bidder managers knowingly pay too much for target firms? J Bus 63 (4):439–464

Shield R, Thorpe R, Nelson A (2002) Hospital mergers and psychological contracts. Strateg Chang 11(7):357–367

Shimuzu K, Hitt M, Vaidyanath D, Pisano V (2004) Theoretical foundations of cross-border mergers and acquisitions: a review of current research and recommendations for the future. J Int Manag 10:307–353

Shrivastava P (1986) Postmerger integration. J Bus Strateg 7(1):65–76

Simon H (1947) Administrative behavior: a study of decision making processes in administrative organizations. Free Press, New York, NY

Simon HA (1964) On the concept of organizational goal. Adm Sci Q 9(1):1–22

Sirmon DG, Hitt MA, Ireland RD (2007) Managing firm resources in dynamic environments to create value: looking inside the black box. Acad Manag Rev 32:273–292

Sirower ML (1997) Synergy trap: how companies lose the acquisition game. Simon & Schuster, New York, NY

Slusky AR, Caves RE (1991) Synergy, agency and the determinants of premia paid in mergers. J Ind Econ 39(3):277–296

Sparks D (1998) Creating and leading strategic combinations. Delta Consulting Group, New York, NY

Stahl GK, Voight A (2008) Do cultural differences matter in mergers and acquisitions? A tentative model for examination. Organ Sci 19:160–176

Stahl GK, Angwin DN, Very P, Gomes E, Weber Y, Tarba SY, Noorderhaven N, Benyamini H, Bouckenooghe D, Chreim S, Durand M, Hassett ME, Kokk G, Mendenhall ME, Mirc N, Miska C, Park KM, Reynolds N-S, Rouzies A, Sarala RM, Seloti SL, Søndergaard M, Yildiz HE (2013) Sociocultural integration in mergers and acquisitions: unresolved paradoxes and directions for future research. Thunderbird Int Bus Rev 55(4):333–356

Steiner PO (1975) Mergers: motives, effect, policies. University of Michigan Press, Ann Arbor, MI

Strikwerda J, Stoelhorst JW (2009) The emergence and evolution of the multidimensional organization. Calif Manag Rev 51(4):11–31

Sudarsanam S, Holl P, Salami A (1996) Shareholder wealth gains in mergers: effect of synergy and ownership. J Bus Financ Account 23(5–6):673–698

Takeishi A (2001) Bridging inter- and intra-firm boundaries: management of supplier involvement in automobile product development. Strateg Manag J 22(5):403–433

Teece DJ, Pisano G, Shuen A (1997) Dynamic capabilities and strategic management. Strateg Manag J 18:509–533

Thanos IC, Papadakis VM (2012) The use of accounting-based measures in measuring M&A performance: a review of five decades of research. In: Cooper CL, Finkelstein S (eds) Advances in mergers and acquisitions, vol 10. Emerald, Bingley

Thompson A et al (2013) Crafting & executing strategy: the quest for competitive advantage: concepts and cases, 19th edn. McGraw-Hill Education, New York, NY

Tortoriello M, Krackhardt D (2010) Activating cross-boundary knowledge: the role of Simmelian ties in the generation of innovations. Acad Manag J 53(1):167–181

Trautwein F (1990) Merger motives and merger prescriptions. Strateg Manag J 11:283–295

Uhlenbruck K, Hitt MA, Semadeni M (2006) Market value effects of acquisitions involving internet firms: a resource based analysis. Strateg Manag J 27(10):899–913

Vaara E (2002) On the discursive construction of success/failure in narratives of post-merger integration. Organ Sci 23(2):211–248

Vaara E (2003) Post-acquisition integration as sensemaking: glimpses of ambiguity, confusion, hypocrisy, and politicization. J Manag Stud 40(4):859–894

Villalonga B, McGahan AM (2005) The choice among acquisitions, alliances, and divestitures. Strateg Manag J 26(13):1183–1208

Vivek S, Banwet D, Shankar R (2008) Analysis of interactions among core, transaction and relationship-specific investments. J Oper Manag 26(2):180–197

Weber Y (2011) Managing mergers and acquisitions: implementation and integration. Int Stud Manag Organ 41(3):3–8

Weber Y (2013) Handbook of research on mergers and acquisitions. Edward Elgar, Cheltenham

Wernefelt B (1995) The resource-based view of the firm: ten years after. Strateg Manag J 16:171–174

Williamson OE (1975) Markets and hierarchies. Free Press, New York, NY

Yu J, Engleman RM, Van de Ven AH (2005) The integration journey: an attention-based view of the merger and acquisition integration process. Organ Stud 26(10):1501–1528

Zaheer A, Castaner X, Souder R (2013) Synergy sources, target autonomy, and integration in acquisitions. J Manag 39(3):604–632

Zollo M, Meier D (2008) What is M&A performance? Acad Manag Perspect 22(3):55–77

Chapter 3
Inside Synergy Assessment: Towards the Real Value of M&As

Abstract This chapter develops an effective synergy assessment model to support the process of synergy valuation and the success of pre-deal planning. The effectiveness of the synergy value depends from the valuation models, the valuation path and the assessment process. We highlight that the synergy assessment process and the effective use of synergy valuation models are critical points to cut the failure rate of mergers and acquisitions. We analyze the most relevant valuation models and the strategic factors affecting synergy: the type of synergy, the size of synergy, the timing of synergy and the likelihood of achievement. The effective use of synergy assessment models is critical to improve the success of mergers and acquisitions due-diligence.

Keywords Mergers • Acquisition • Synergy value • Assessment process • Valuation models • Due-diligence

3.1 The Value of Synergy

The assessment of synergy value is a relevant issue in the M&A decision process. From the value of synergy often depends whether to complete or not the deal. Consequently, firms may provide estimation on synergy value to verify the effectiveness of the proposed M&A and to persuade stockholders and stakeholders (Ansoff 1965; Campa and Hernando 2004; Chatterjee 1992; Kiymaz and Baker 2008).

Previous studies do not univocally use synergy value. A closer look reveals that the term is characterized by a strong depth of thought often by highly technical features (Latash 2008). Scholars have distinguished synergy expectations and synergy realizations, often neglecting the relationship between the two. Furthermore, scholars have often forgotten that it is costly to integrate firms in mergers and acquisitions (Datta 1991; Zhou 2011). Attempting to integrate several approaches, we can refer to synergy as the difference between the stand alone value of firms involved in M&A and the greater value of firms after M&A.

Based on this notion, we can discriminate several "values": "potential synergy", the overall synergies that can be developed by the deal; "integration costs", the costs needed to realize the synergies by integrating the firms; "expected synergy",

S. Garzella, R. Fiorentino, *Synergy Value and Strategic Management*, Contributions to Management Science, DOI 10.1007/978-3-319-40671-8_3

the synergy value assessed from firms in the due-diligence process; and "realized synergy", the value actually achieved after the M&A integration (Garzella and Fiorentino 2014). "Synergy value" results from the difference between the potential synergy and the integration costs (Eccles et al. 1999; Fiorentino and Garzella 2015a, b).

When the synergy management process is effective—in both the assessment and the realization steps—the synergy value can be seen as follows:

$$SV = RS = ES = (PS - IC)$$

SV Synergy value
ES Expected synergy
PS Potential synergy
IC Integration costs
RS Realized synergy

The prior synergy values should be further analyzed with respect to additional perspectives (Fig. 3.1).

Based on value creation theories (Rappaport 1986; Demirakos et al. 2004) and synergy studies (e.g., Damodaran 2005), it is possible to argue that the value of synergy expectations depends on the financial flows related to the potential M&A synergies, on their temporal distribution, and on the discount rate. Consistently, the improvement of the performance delivered by synergies is the present value of net additional financial flows generated by the deal that firms could not produce without the merger itself (Damodaran 2005; Demirakos et al. 2004). The synergistic effects could produce an improvement in the performance of the merged firms through increased revenues, cost savings, risk reduction, and an abatement of financial needs. The value creation theory suggests to give autonomous importance to the form of forecasted synergy (Gupta and Gerchak 2002) in order to represent specific dimensions of strategy and organisational structures. According to this approach, the synergy value is the present value of the expected synergy flows deriving from the deal, discounted back at a rate that reflects the riskiness of these flows. In order to assess the individual synergy flows in a deal firms should calculate specific future synergy flows, and the effects of M&A on both risk levels and financial needs.

One of the main challenges in M&A is developing a pre-acquisition decision process that indicates which is the potential synergy value, even under conditions of incomplete information, rapidity and secretiveness (Evans and Bishop 2001). In other words, firms must assess the synergy value to find true value-creating acquisitions (Sirower 2003).

However, the assessment of synergy value is a complex process which should provide both a qualitative analysis and a quantitative measurement. The qualitative step should analyses the strategic factors affecting synergy whilst the quantitative step should turn strategic factors in synergy value.

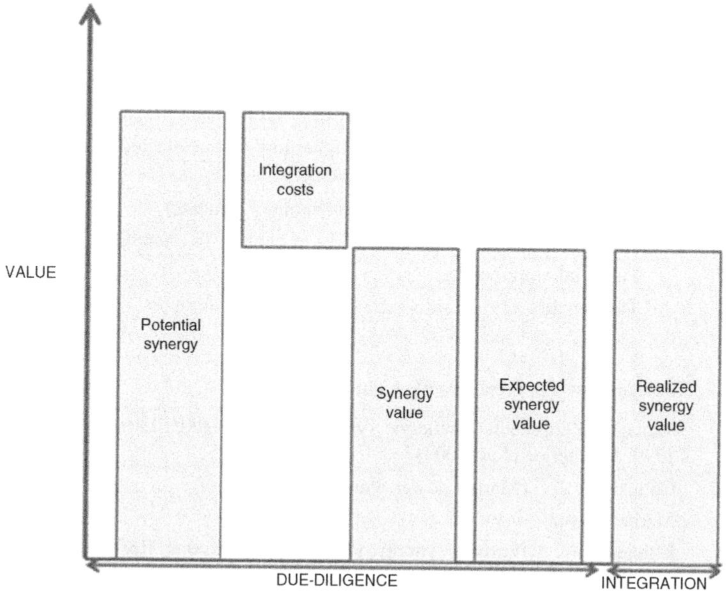

Fig. 3.1 Synergy value

3.2 The Analysis of Strategic Factors Affecting Synergy

The effectiveness of synergy value assessment process first depends from the analysis of M&A strategic factors (Garzella and Fiorentino 2014). The strategic factors, that are considered very relevant to generating reliable forecasts, should be adequately quantified by answering questions, such as: What is the expected form of the synergy? What is the expected size of the synergy? When does the synergy start affecting earnings and cash flows? What is the likelihood of achievement of each synergy type? (e.g., Damodaran 2005).

3.2.1 What Is the Expected Form of the Synergy?

The starting point of the analysis is related to the expected form of synergy. An in-depth review of studies in M&A, integrating the most relevant articles published in leading management, accounting and finance journals over the last 30 years, show that scholars categorize synergy in many ways. By integrating the insights from prior studies, it is possible to identify three main approaches: one, widespread in Anglo-Saxon studies, where synergies are analysed based on cost-saving expectations and on revenue growth opportunities; a second, common in European studies, where, although categorisations are rarely coincident, a common matrix

Table 3.1 The revenue/cost approach to the nature of synergy

	Revenue/costs approach (Bruner 2004; Eccles et al. 1999; Evans and Bishop 2001)	
Synergy form	Cost saving	(Positions, Overhead, Related fixed asset)
	Revenue enhancements	(Higher unit sales, Selected rice increases)
	Process improvements	
	Practice improvements	(Technology, Process)
	Financial economies	(Cost of capital, Tax benefits)
	Financial engineering	
	Tax benefits	

Table 3.2 The managerial approach to the nature of synergy

	Managerial approach (Chatterjee 1986; Damodaran 2005; Larsson and Finkelstein 1999; Mukherjee et al. 2004)	
Synergy form	Collusive	(Market power, Purchasing power)
	Market power	
	Efficiency	(Growth synergy, Production, Marketing, R&D, Administration, Economies of staircases, Tax, Financing, Debt capacity)
	Operating	
	Managerial	(Applying complementary competencies, Replacing incompetent managers)
	Financial	(Cost of capital, Tax benefits, Excess cash or cash slack, Risk diversification, Coinsurance)
	Dubious	(Accretive acquisitions, Quick growth)

can be detected in the research of synergy nature; and a third that constitutes a mix of the other two approaches (Tables 3.1, 3.2, and 3.3).

In the "European approach", which adopts a managerial perspective based on the typical statements of accruals and financial flows, the nature of synergies and their related flows may be analysed in relation to three areas: operations, synergies that allow firms to increase their operating income; finances, synergies that decrease the financing costs; taxation, synergies that produce tax benefits.

For instance, an empirical investigation by Accenture (2007) showed that synergy expectations are not adequately valorised because they are usually only generally identified and described. Another survey by KPMG (1999) concluded that "direct operational cost reductions" are the most important type of synergy with a rate of 39 %; "revenue benefits" have an importance of 36 %; "indirect overhead cost reduction" represents 9 % of the overall value of the synergy expectations; and the other types of synergies together account for the remaining 16 %. Finally, McKinsey's research in the IT sector found that, on average, the revenue growth decreases following a M&A deal (Bekier and Shelton 2002).

Anyhow, an accurate analysis of expected size, not only of total synergy but also with reference to each synergy type, is fundamental in any synergy assessment in M&A.

Table 3.3 The mixed approach to the nature of synergy

	Mixed approach (Goold and Campbell 1998; Harding and Rovit 2005; Haspeslagh and Jemison 1991)	
Synergy form	Shared know how	
	Shared tangible resources	
	Pooled negotiations	
	Coordinated strategies	
	Vertical integration	
	Combined business creation	
	Elimination of the duplication	
	Sharing of the operational costs	
	Rationalization installs	
	Synergies of proceeds	(Existing product through new channels, New product through new channels)
	The common use of the operational resources	
	Transfer of the functional competence and general direction	
	Due benefits to the combinations	

3.2.2 *When Does the Synergy Starts Affecting Earnings and Cash-Flows?*

Two factors make timing particularly important in the measurement of synergy expectations: its impact on the likelihood of achievement (Allred et al. 2005; Angwin 2004; Harding and Rovit 2005) and its influence on the discount value (Evans and Bishop 2001; Deloitte 2007).

With regard to the former, several studies have found that synergy achievement becomes increasingly difficult over time (Bert et al. 2003; Haspeslagh and Jemison 1991; Hintherhuber 2002). Whereas some of them suggest that the temporal lag between closing and the start of integration "has the strongest and most negative effect on the acquisition performance" (Colombo et al. 2007: 215), other studies argue that the speed of the integration can positively or negatively influence the success of M&A deals (Homburg and Bucerius 2006). In this context, some trade-offs may generally emerge between the possibility of realising lower short-term synergy flows and the opportunity for higher but long-term benefits. With reference to the latter reason for the importance of timing, value creation theory argues that, if all other conditions are equal, the value of synergies is negatively correlated to the timing of their realisation (Copeland 1994; Rappaport 1986).

Although, as Eccles et al. (1999) suggest, firms often underestimate the time needed for the realisation of synergies, the effect of timing on synergy value should be adequately considered in M&A process.

3.2.3 What Is the Likelihood of Achievement of Each Synergy Type?

Ambiguity of expectations, representing one of the main decisional problems in M&A, make the likelihood of synergy achievement a relevant factor for the depth of synergy measurement (Cullinan et al. 2004; Damodaran 2005; Evans and Bishop 2001).

In the literature, the likelihood of achievement of a synergy is generally related to the ease of its realisation. In academic research, many studies have measured the degree of synergy achievement with reference to the features of both the firms involved and the realised M&A, although their results have not always been consistent. For example, some scholars have suggested (Bradley et al. 1988) that the success of a deal is positively correlated to the degree of relatedness of the involved firms; however, others have found that the likelihood of success is greater in unrelated mergers (Lubatkin 1987; Harrison et al. 1991). Finally, a few studies have analysed the likelihood of achieving different types of synergies based on specific characteristics of M&A deals, such as horizontal/non-horizontal, related/unrelated or complementary/similar (Chatterjee 1986; Zaheer et al. 2013).

On the practitioners' side, surveys conducted by advisors and consultants have demonstrated different levels of achievement between revenue growth and cost-saving synergies. Specifically, the likelihood of success of each type of synergies depends on both the difficulty of assessment and the intensity of implementation efforts. However, the evidence remains ambiguous. For instance, Harding and Rovit (2005) argue that cost-saving synergies are easier to realise. However, in a survey by Accenture (2007), only half of the respondents affirmed that their expectations on revenue growth synergy had been achieved and only 45 % of them declared that their expectations for cost savings had been met (Accenture 2007). Similarly, the results of McKinsey's study found that more than the 40 % of M&A deals do not meet expectations in terms of cost-saving benefits (Bekier and Shelton 2002).

Then, the estimation of the likelihood is very relevant. The likelihood of achieving synergy in M&As is related to the ease of realisation of different synergy types: the ease of realisation is the reciprocal of the likelihood of achievement. Operating synergies have generally the lowest likelihood of achievement, instead tax synergies have the highest. Cost synergies are more likely to be achieved than revenue synergies.

This is related mainly to the optimisation of a trade-off between the accuracy and quantity of data and the time needed for M&A integration. Thus, it is necessary to decide between an objective and quick analysis with limited significance or a highly subjective and time-intensive analysis using more meaningful data. This choice is very important in the exploitation of the synergies because they are not all equally identifiable, achievable, and evaluable (Eccles et al. 1999; Hamel and Prahalad 1995).

The estimated synergy value is a function of the analyzed factors and the specific valuation models used as primary and control models. Thus, "net present valuation", according to the analytic approach, in particular appears to be more appropriate than other paths and models for translating qualitative analysis into quantitative synergy value. The latter estimates the real value of M&A, allowing firms to avoid "false positive" deals. Overall, the timing, size and likelihood of achievement of synergy, estimated through valuation models, mediate the assessment of synergy value.

3.3 The Synergy Valuation Models

Prior research about mergers and acquisitions (M&A) underlines the importance of the pre-acquisition phase, when the M&A's contribution to the overarching corporate strategy and its price are still under evaluation. Specifically, in the assessment process it is fundamental to assess the risks of a bad valuation of synergy (Bruner 2002; Haspeslagh and Jemison 1991; Rappaport and Sirower 1999). Therefore, it is necessary to extend previous models to further the assessment of synergy expectations in the pre-acquisition phase of M&A agreements, which are a key element for the success of M&A deals (Garzella and Fiorentino 2014; KPMG 1999). In this respect, Sirower (1997) observes that synergies are often promised but seldom realised. Furthermore, research shows that two-thirds of the executives involved in M&A agreements believe that they have overestimated the value of synergy expectations and that their error has substantially driven the failures of the deals (Harding and Rovit 2005).

Thus, a key question is how synergies should be evaluated and how firms may avoid risks of potential synergy misassessment (Damodaran 2005)?

The assessment of the synergy value is regarded as one of the most critical points in M&A (Larsson and Finkelstein 1999; Martinez-Jerez 2008), and the relative usefulness of various company valuation models has been the subject of considerable empirical research in recent years (Arnold and Mozier 1984; Barker 1999; Block 1999; Lundholm and O'Keefe 2001; Penman 2001). These studies are often focused on a comparison of residual income-based accounting valuation models and DCF (discounted cash flows) models (Penman and Sougiannis 1998; Francis et al. 2000; Courteau et al. 2001). These theoretically equivalent valuation models (i.e., residual income and DCF) are sometimes compared to the relatively "unsophisticated" valuation models (i.e., multiples models) that are increasingly being used by practitioners (Imam et al. 2008).

With reference to synergy, it is possible to highlight two main valuation models in which theories and approaches from accounting and financial analysis converge (Garzella and Fiorentino 2014). The first, the "net present value" model, gives autonomous importance to each type of synergy that appears in financial flows (Gupta and Gerchak 2002; Rappaport 1986). The second, the "relative valuation" model, identifies particular multiples based on empirical values that aim to quantify the value of synergies (Gupta and Gerchak 2002; Liu et al. 2002).

Because a strategy may be evaluated through the potential modifications of firm value that it generates, it is suitable to reference the "value creation theory" (Copeland 1994; Rappaport 1986) in the synergy assessment. Based on a preliminary content analysis of M&A reports and a selection of academic studies and accounting and finance tests, it is possible to highlight two main valuation models and two paths in which theories and approaches from strategic management converge with those typical of the accounting and finance analysis of synergies (Brealey and Myers 2003; Damodaran 2005; Demirakos et al. 2004; Frankel and Lee 1998).

The first model, the "net present value" model, gives autonomous importance to each type of synergy that appears in forecasts (Biddle et al. 1997; Gupta and Gerchak 2002) and is generally considered appropriate for representing specific dimensions of corporate strategy and organisational structure (Nurnberg 2006). According to this approach, the synergy value is the present value of the expected synergy flows from the deal process, discounted back at a rate that reflects the riskiness of these flows. In our analysis, this approach includes models based on both earnings and cash flow metrics. Indeed, it is not relevant in our research whether valuations are based on cash flows or accruals, but it is important to know how forecasts are provided.

The second model, the "relative valuation" model, values synergies based upon how similarly they are priced in the market (Damodaran 2005; Gupta and Gerchak 2002; Liu et al. 2002). According to this model, the synergy value is obtained by comparing the expected synergy flows to a specific variable taken as a constant for similar firms or deals. In our analysis, this approach includes models based on both multiples and comparable transactions.

The models may be applied according to the analytic or the synthetic approaches. The synthetic approach aims to assess the overall value of synergy. According to this model, the synergy value, that is, the surplus value created by an M&A process, is indirectly calculated without any assessment of single synergies. The analytic approach, instead, aims to assess the individual synergy flows in a deal by calculating specific future synergy flows (Table 3.4).

Specifically, models based on the net present value of financial flows are most effective for both theoretical and empirical research (Baker et al. 1981; Mohan et al. 1991; Mukherjee et al. 2004; Villalonga 2004).

Far from being antithetical and mutually exclusive, the several valuation models can be jointly applied for their mutual confirmation and to gain more information and increase accuracy by combining the different peculiarities and strengths characterising each model. Indeed, in practice, the valuation obtained using a primary model is compared with the valuations from one or more control models.

Table 3.4 Major synergy valuation models

Model	Main version	Path	Definition
Net present valuation	Discounted cash flow (DCF)	Analytic	Relates the synergy value to the present value of synergy flows expected from the deals
		Synthetic	Relates the synergy value to the difference between the present value of cash flows of both firms and the present value of the cash flows of the combined firm
	Discounted future earnings (DFE)	Analytic	Relates the synergy value to the present value of future synergy earnings
		Synthetic	Relates the synergy value to the difference between the present value of future earnings of both firms and the present value of future earnings of the combined firm
Relative valuation	Multiple model	Analytic	Relates the synergy value to the product of synergy flows and a common variable taken as a constant for comparable firms
		Synthetic	Relates the synergy value to the difference between the multiple values of the combined firm exceeding the value from the two independent firms
	Comparable transactions model	Analytic	Relates the synergy value to the product of synergy flows and a common variable taken as a constant for comparable transactions
		Synthetic	Relates the synergy value to the synergy value from comparable transactions

3.4 The Assessment of Synergy Value

Qualitative analyses would be reduced to mere discursive exercises without the support of quantitative measurements, and the latter would constitute technical bookkeeping exercises without the former to confer significance to the valuation (Barker 1999). Business valuations may be based on prior strategic analysis of the deal that requires forecasting post-merger cash flows according to the planned post-merger strategy (Cormier and Magnan 2005; Zollo and Meier 2008). Only analytic valuation models require the assessment of strategic factors. Therefore, to identify the synergy value that will be achieved, using an analytical approach, the type, weight, timing and ease of realisation of each synergy must be considered. The strategic factors that influence the value assessment of synergy are as follows (Accenture 2007; Barkema and Schijven 2008; Barker 1999; Damodaran 2005; Evans and Bishop 2001; Garzella and Fiorentino 2014; Harding and Rovit 2005):

- Synergy form;
- Synergy size;
- Synergy timing;
- Likelihood of achievement.

In the pre-deal decision-making, the assessment process should start from the analysis of synergy form. First, an examination of "what" is the synergy nature is useful, distinguishing operating synergies from financial and tax synergies. Second, executives should forecast "how" these synergies will arise in terms of higher revenues or lower costs. Third, the assessment process should clarify "where" synergistic flows may be allocated: at one SBU or at the corporate level. It is advisable to develop the analysis of synergy form in the initial stage because the form of synergy differently affects the other three factors: the size, the timing and the likelihood of achievement (Hayward 2002; Ahuja and Katila 2001). Operating synergies generally have broader effects than financial and tax synergies. Cost operating, financial and tax synergies generally require less time than revenue operating synergies do. Indeed, the timing of synergy affects its size and likelihood of achievement. Synergies improve firms' performance by means of revenue growth, cost savings, or reduced levels of risk and financial need (Damodaran 2005).

These reflections suggests to simultaneously analyze the size, the timing and the likelihood of achievement in the second stage of the synergy measurement process (Garzella and Fiorentino 2014). The examination of synergy size should push to the quantification of synergistic flows related to each synergy type. The investigation of timing and likelihood of realization should support the assessment of the discount rate of prior synergistic flows (Fig. 3.2).

With respect to the nature of the synergy, we should distinguish among the concepts of operating, financial and tax synergies (Capron et al. 1998; Garzella 2006; Goold and Campbell 2000). Specifically, operating synergies can be based on sharing resources and processes (e.g., sales networks, manufacturing plants, research laboratories, materials, etc.). These synergies can change the conditions of a company's profitability in the following situations: (1) when the commonality of activities allows for sharing expenses and structural factors or efforts to increase the cumulative volume of operational activities of the same type, resulting in cost savings based on economies of scale (Porter 1980); (2) when there is a more intense exploitation (Barney and Arikan 2001) of the available operational capabilities (manufacturing, logistics, research & development, procurement, etc.); (3) when higher revenues are ensured as a result of scope economies derived from the increased accumulation of skills and the character of the products' uniqueness/superiority; and (4) when the incidence of diversification costs is reduced because of the distribution of those costs across a larger number of products. Indeed, synergies are related to the ability to use the same skills and knowledge (marketing, technical, scientific, logistic, administrative, etc.) through the transfer of distinctive capabilities and exclusive powers from one company to another, allowing those companies to boost and complement their technical and managerial know-how (Ensign 1998; Goold and Campbell 1998) (Fig. 3.3).

However, this categorisation is not sufficient: sub-categorisations should be used, especially for operating synergy. These sub-categorisations should be primarily based on strategic models and tools but also finance and accounting models

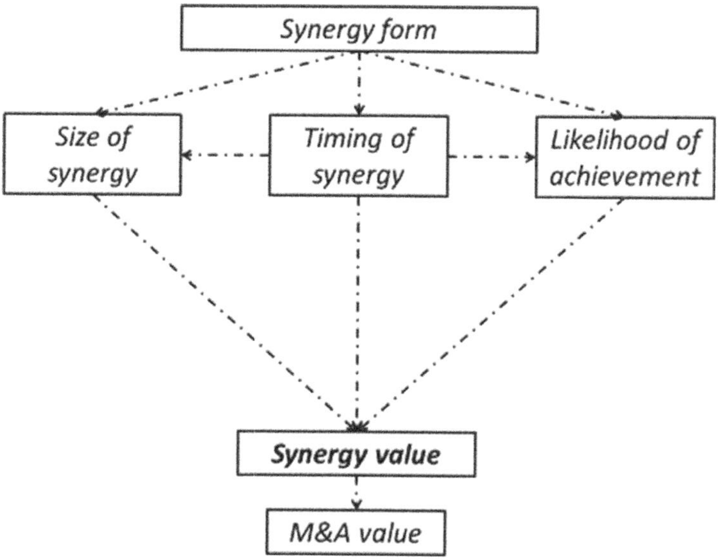

Fig. 3.2 A synergy assessment model

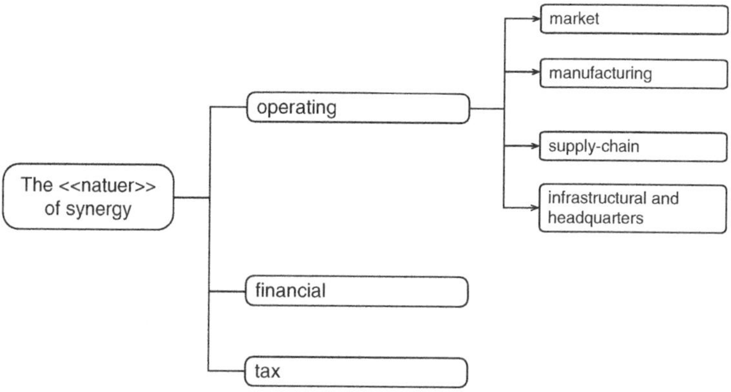

Fig. 3.3 Synergy form: by nature

are useful. Firms, advisors and consultants should integrate different approaches available in the literature to make synergy assessment more effective.

Some synergies are related to "market" issues, whereas others are related to manufacturing and supply processes. By sharing resources, processes, and customers, M&A deals aim to increase products' volumes and prices on the revenue-enhancement side and to optimize volumes and unitary costs of inputs on the cost-savings side. The source of "market" synergies is the possibility of serving the same customers with several products that complement one another to increase overall profitability. Integrative actions may aim to obtain both outcomes at the same time

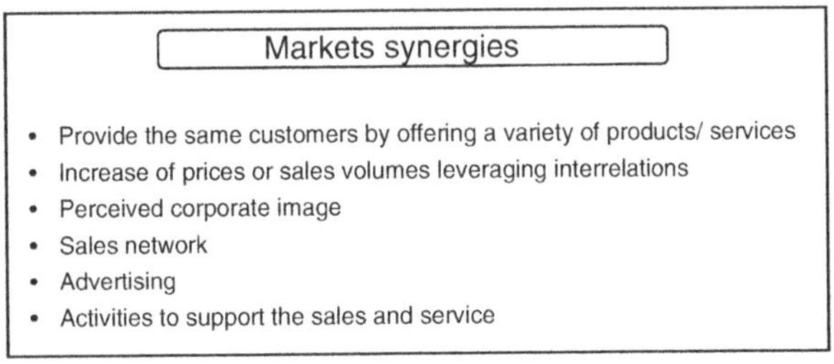

Fig. 3.4 Market synergies

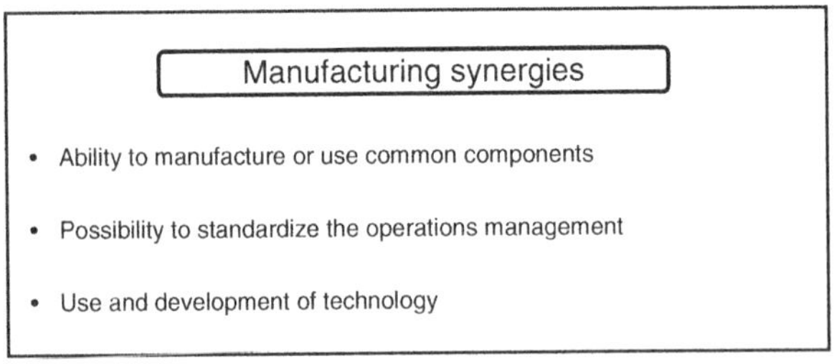

Fig. 3.5 Manufacturing synergies

by exploiting synergies in customer perceptions, sales networks, or advertising (Fig. 3.4).

Other studies focus on the "manufacturing side" (Fig. 3.5). Synergies arise out of the ability to produce or use the same components and the ability to optimize supply chain or IT systems (Fig. 3.6).

Indeed, firms may achieve supply-chain synergies by centralizing purchases and achieving better input quality, timing and cost. Similarly, firms may develop infrastructural and headquarters synergies by jointly managing common support activities such as human resources management (Fig. 3.7).

On the financial and tax sides, synergy is created to reduce financing costs by sharing financial resources, exploiting possible cash flow asynchronicities among different strategic business units, and decreasing taxation (Porter Liebeskind 2000).

These synergies can be achieved primarily by reducing risk levels, decreasing the cost of debt capital, limiting the total amount of funding, increasing lending capacity, and improving knowledge of financial markets. In this way, firms may reduce both their global financial needs and their costs (Fig. 3.8).

For example, an important component of financial synergies is the ability to reduce the risk of diversification by applying logic based on the creation of a corporate portfolio, although this logic is not sustainable as a strategic driver in manufacturing firms because financial firms, such as investment funds, will always be more efficient and effective in exploiting diversification strategies (Mathur and Kenyon 1998).

Finally, tax synergies (Fig. 3.9) aim to decrease taxation pressures on firms (Copeland 1994) by reducing taxable income and tax band (Copeland 1994; Devos et al. 2009).

Supply-chain synergies

- Centralized procurement management
- Better conditions for the acquisition of production factors in terms of quality, timing and costs.

Fig. 3.6 Supply-chain synergies

Infrastructure and headquaters synergies

Common management of infrastructure:
- Human resources management
- Administration
- Legal offices
- etc.

Fig. 3.7 Infrastructure and headquarters synergies

Financial synergies

Optimize the financial resources:
- Increase borrowing capacity
- Asynchronies in financial flows
- Reduced portfolio risk
- Decrease in the costs of debts
- Reduction in the total amount of funding

Fig. 3.8 Financial synergies

Tax synergies

- Benefit from tax credits formed in the financial statements as a result of operating losses
- Access to subsidized loans
- "Tax shield"

Fig. 3.9 Tax synergies

Moreover firms should analyse the "area" where the synergies are allocated: at the corporate, the division or the Strategic Business Unit (SBU) level. This categorisation is relevant because it affects the magnitude and the likelihood of achievement of synergy (Garzella and Fiorentino 2014). Although synergies

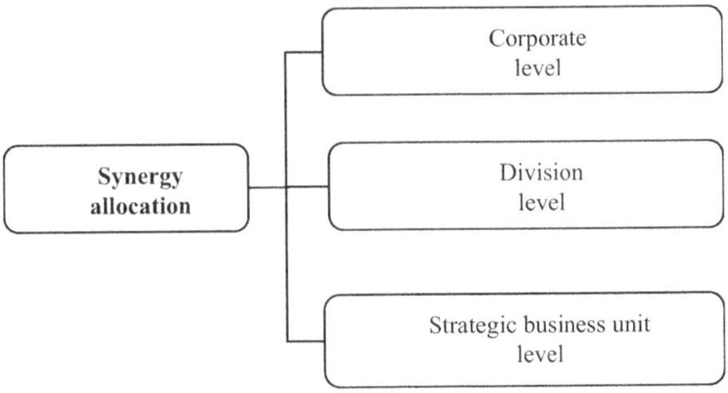

Fig. 3.10 The "area" of synergy allocation

develop at the corporate level, operating synergies can be observed, and consequently measured, at various levels. The market, manufacturing and supply synergies are generally created at the business level, but they could also develop at the corporate level; in the reorganisation of mixed structures, operating and infrastructural activities are placed and centralised at the corporate level (e.g., purchasing, research, technology, some manufacturing steps, and advertising); in multidivisional organizations, some of the prior operating synergies generally show up at divisional level (e.g. the cost savings from sharing a plant between two SBUs). The infrastructural synergies are generally placed at the divisional or corporate level. It should also be highlighted that operating synergies, in particular, can occur in several SBUs, but if they are not infrastructural, they cannot be assigned to each SBU exclusively. Instead, their value is created by the firm as a whole after the M&A (Fig. 3.10).

In the analysis of synergy size, consistent with the previous literature, firms have to consider that the operating synergies are among the main determinants of M&As. The M&A value is created primarily through the realisation of operating synergies, supported by financial synergies, which are also an important managerial lever. Tax synergies appear to be almost entirely unimportant for value creation, if only for the increasingly compelling reason of avoiding evasion; however, tax synergies seem to have a remarkable impact in turnaround strategies. In summary, it is not misleading to argue that synergy value is created primarily in the operational businesses and in their interrelations. However, the financial and tax synergies are able to supplement the operating synergies, but they are not the main strategic aim.

In the analysis of synergy timing, firms should avoid a substantial inconsistency among the time frames for synergy realisation and their respect because firms generally underestimate the time needed to realise synergy (Bert et al. 2003; Schweiger et al. 1987). The common expected timing of M&A operations, in average between 3 and 5 years, is a remarkable factor *ex-ante* when synergies are assessed during the decision process. The assessment of the time is a very relevant factor related to the synergy types and able to affect both the likelihood of achievement and the synergy size.

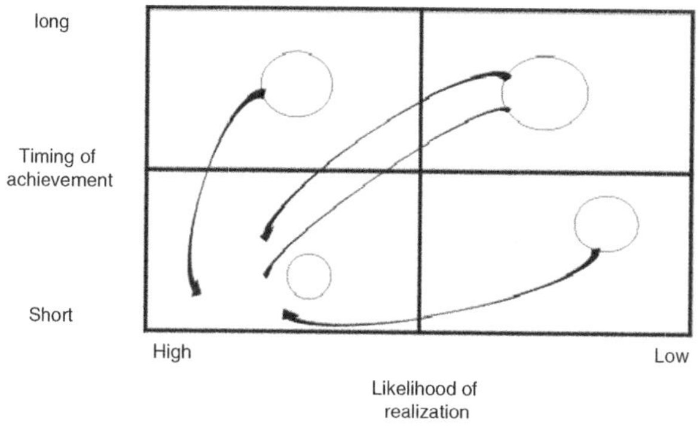

Fig. 3.11 The matrix "Timing of achievement-Likelihood of realization". The size of the circular spaces in the matrix represents the size of several synergies. The synergy management should "push" synergies toward the corner at the bottom left. The *arrows* suggest possible paths, shown by exemplificative ways, since synergy achievement should follow multiple trajectories and even occur trade-off between the likelihood and timing

However, the assessment of the timing of the synergy is sometimes affected by contextual factors and external pressures. Valuation processes assume short durations that imply a lower discount rate and a higher synergy value. Indeed, the assessment and the respect of deadlines are related to the synergy types, as traditionally deadlines are easier to respect with reference to financial and tax synergies but not for operating synergies. Because the timing affects the value creation of the deal, timing itself may be one cause of the reduced creation of value by M&As demonstrated in several previous studies (Fig. 3.11).

After completing the analysis of strategic factors, firms have information to assess the synergy value. We suggest the use of sophisticated valuation models (Imam et al. 2008) and a preference for "net present value" models in mergers and acquisitions (Mukherjee et al. 2004). However, other types of models, such as accounting models, are also used in practice (Demirakos et al. 2004). Indeed, there is widespread consensus on the simultaneous use of different models as control models, consistent with earlier research suggesting that valuation models are complementary to each other and more relevant in combination (Barker 1999). The most frequently mentioned reasons for the use of a particular model are technical considerations related to the data needed for the effective use of the model and the theoretical foundations of the model.

Anyhow, all of the tools that are useful to facilitate the passage from the qualitative analyses to those that are "value based" should be used, articulating the connection between the strategic analysis and the valuation models: synergy assessment cannot be separated from value estimation (Garzella and Fiorentino 2014).

References

Accenture (2007) Strategy in action. The synergy enigma. http://www.accenture.com

Ahuja G, Katila A (2001) Technological acquisition and the innovation performance of acquiring firms: a longitudinal study. Strateg Manag J 22(3):197–220

Allred BB, Boal KB, Holstein WK (2005) Corporations as stepfamilies: a new metaphor for explaining the fate of merged and acquired companies. Acad Manag Exec 19(3):23–37

Angwin D (2004) Speed in M&A integration: the first 100 days. Eur Manag J 22(4):418–430

Ansoff HI (1965) Corporate strategy. McGraw-Hill, New York, NY

Arnold JA, Mozier P (1984) A survey of the methods used by UK investments analysts to appraise investments in ordinary shares. Account Bus Res 14(55):195–207

Baker HK, Miller TO, Ramsperger BJ (1981) An inside look at corporate mergers and acquisitions. MSU Bus Top 29(1):49–57

Barkema HG, Schijven M (2008) Toward unlocking the full potential of acquisitions. Acad Manag J 51(4):696–722

Barker RG (1999) The role of dividends in valuation models used by analysts and fund managers. Eur Account Rev 8:195–218

Barney J, Arikan A (2001) The resource-based view: origins and implications. In: Hitt MA, Freeman E, Harrison J (eds) The Blackwell handbook of strategic management. Blackwell Business, Oxford, UK, pp 124–188

Bekier MM, Shelton MJ (2002) Keeping your sales force after the merger. McKinsey Q 12 (4):106–115

Bert A, MacDonald T, Herd T (2003) Two merger integration imperatives: urgency and execution. Strateg Leadersh 31(3):42–49

Biddle GC, Bowen RM, Wallace JS (1997) Does EVA® beat earnings? Evidence on associations with stock returns and firm values. J Account Econ 24(3):301–336

Block SB (1999) A study of financial analysts: practice and theory. Financ Anal J 55(4):86–95

Bradley M, Desai A, Kim HE (1988) Synergistic gains from corporate acquisitions and their divisions between the stockholders of target and acquiring firms. J Financ Econ 21(1):3–40

Brealey RA, Myers SC (2003) Principles of corporate finance. McGraw-Hill, New York, NY

Bruner RF (2002) Does M&A pay? A survey of evidence for the decision maker. J Appl Financ Theory Pract Educ 12(1):48–88

Bruner RF (2004) Deals from hell: M&A lessons that rise above the ashes. Wiley, New York, NY

Campa JM, Hernando I (2004) Shareholder value creation in European M&A. Eur Financ Manag 10:47–81

Capron L, Dussauge P, Mitchell W (1998) Resource redeployment following horizontal acquisitions in Europe and North America 1988-1992. Strateg Manag J 19(7):631–661

Chatterjee S (1986) Types of synergy and economic value: the impact of acquisitions on merging and rival firms. Strateg Manag J 7(2):119–139

Chatterjee S (1992) Sources of value in takeovers: synergy or restructuring-implications for target and bidder firms. Strateg Manag J 13(4):267–286

Colombo G, Conca V, Buongiorno M, Gnan L (2007) Integrating cross-border acquisitions: a process-oriented approach. Long Range Plan 40(2):202–222

Copeland T (1994) Why value value? McKinsey Q 4:97–109

Cormier D, Magnan ML (2005) From accounting to "Forecounting". Can Account Perspect 4 (2):243–255

Courteau L, Kao J, Richardson G (2001) Equity valuation employing the ideal versus ad hoc terminal value expressions. Contemp Account Res 18(4):625–661

Cullinan G, Le Roux J, Weddigen R (2004) When to walk away from a deal. Harv Bus Rev 82 (4):96–105

Damodaran A (2005) The value of synergy. Stern School of Business, New York, NY, SSRN 841486(2005)

Datta DK (1991) Organizational fit and acquisition performance: effects of post-acquisition integration. Strateg Manag J 12(4):281–297
Deloitte (2007) Strategic acquisitions amid business uncertainty. http://www.deloitte.com
Demirakos EG, Strong N, Walker M (2004) What valuation models do analysts use? Account Horiz 18(4):221–240
Devos E, Kadapakkam P, Krishnamurthy S (2009) A comparison of taxes, market power, and efficiency improvements as explanations for synergies. Rev Financ Stud 22(3):1179–1211
Eccles RG, Lanes KL, Wilson TC (1999) Are you paying too much for that acquisition? Harv Bus Rev 77(4):136–146
Ensign PC (1998) Interrelationships and horizontal strategy to achieve synergy and competitive advantage in the diversified firm. Manag Decis 36(10):657–668
Evans FC, Bishop DM (2001) Valuation for M&A: building value in private companies. Wiley, New York, NY
Fiorentino R, Garzella S (2015a) Synergy pitfalls management in mergers and acquisitions. Manag Decis 53(7):1469–1501
Fiorentino R, Garzella S (2015b) The synergy valuation models: towards the real value of mergers and acquisitions. Int Res J Financ Econ 124:71–82
Francis J, Olsson P, Oswald D (2000) Comparing the accuracy and explainability of dividend, free cash flow, and abnormal earnings equity value estimates. J Account Res 38(1):45–70
Frankel R, Lee CMC (1998) Accounting valuation, market expectations, and cross-sectional stock returns. J Account Econ 25(3):283–319
Garzella S (2006) Il governo delle sinergie. Giappichelli, Torino
Garzella S, Fiorentino R (2014) A synergy measurement model to support the pre-deal decision making in mergers and acquisitions. Manag Decis 52(6):1194–1216
Goold M, Campbell A (1998) Desperately seeking synergy. Harv Bus Rev 76:131–143
Goold M, Campbell A (2000) Taking stock of synergy. A framework for assessing linkages between business. Long Range Plan 33:72–96
Gupta D, Gerchak Y (2002) Quantifying operational synergies in a merger/acquisition. Manag Sci 18:517–533
Hamel G, Prahalad CK (1995) Competing for the future. Harvard Business School Press, Cambridge, MA
Harding D, Rovit S (2005) Mastering the merger: four critical decisions that make or break the deal. Harvard Business School Press, Boston, MA
Harrison JS, Hitt MA, Hoskisson RE, Ireland RD (1991) Synergies and post-acquisition performance: differences versus similarities in resource allocations. J Manag 17(1):173–190
Haspeslagh PC, Jemison DB (1991) Managing acquisitions. Free Press, New York, NY
Hayward MLA (2002) When do firms learn from their acquisition experience? Evidence from 1990-1995. Strateg Manag J 23(1):21–39
Hintherhuber HH (2002) Taking time to integrate temporal research. Acad Manag Rev 27(2):170
Homburg C, Bucerius M (2006) Is speed of integration really a success factor of mergers and acquisitions? An analysis of the role of internal and external relatedness. Strateg Manage J 27 (4):347–367
Imam S, Barker R, Clubb C (2008) The use of valuation models by UK investment analysts. Eur Account Rev 17(3):503–535
Kiymaz H, Baker HK (2008) Short-term performance, industry effects, and motives: evidence from large M&As. Q J Financ Account 47(2):17–44
KPMG (1999) Unlocking shareholder value: the keys to success. KPMG, London
Larsson R, Finkelstein S (1999) Integrating strategic, organizational, and human resource perspectives on mergers and acquisitions: a case survey of synergy realization. Organ Sci 10 (1):1–26
Latash ML (2008) Synergy. Oxford University Press, New York, NY
Liu J, Nissim D, Thomas J (2002) Equity valuation using multiples. J Account Res 40(1):135–172
Lubatkin M (1987) Merger strategies and stockholder value. Strateg Manag J 8(1):39–53

Lundholm RJ, O'Keefe T (2001) Reconciling value estimates from the discounted cash flow model and the residual income model. Contemp Account Res 18(2):311–335
Martinez-Jerez FA (2008) Governance and merger accounting: evidence from stock price reactions to purchase versus pooling. Eur Account Rev 17(1):5–35
Mathur SS, Kenyon A (1998) Creating value. Shaping tomorrow's business. Butterwoth-Heinemann, Oxford, UK
Mohan N, Ainina MF, Kaufman D, Winger BJ (1991) Acquisition/divestiture valuation practices in major US firms. Financ Pract Educ 1(1):73–82
Mukherjee TK, Kiymaz H, Baker K (2004) Merger motives and target valuation: a survey of evidence from CFOs. J Appl Financ 14(2):7–24
Nurnberg H (2006) The distorting effects of acquisitions and dispositions on net operating cash flow. Account Forum 30(3):209–226
Penman SH (2001) On comparing cash flow and accrual models for use in equity valuation. Contemp Account Res 18(4):681–692
Penman SH, Sougiannis T (1998) A comparison of dividend, cash flow and earnings approach to equity valuation. Contemp Account Res 15(3):343–383
Porter ME (1980) Competitive strategy. Free Press, New York, NY
Porter Liebeskind J (2000) Internal capital markets: benefits, costs, and organizational arrangements. Org Sci 11(1):58–76
Rappaport A (1986) Creating shareholder value: the new standard for business performance. Free Press, New York, NY
Rappaport A, Sirower ML (1999) Stock or cash? The trade-offs for buyers and sellers in mergers and acquisitions. Harv Bus Rev 77(6):147–158
Schweiger DM, Ivancevich JM, Frank R (1987) Power executive actions for managing human resources before and after acquisition. Acad Manag Exec 1(2):127–138
Sirower ML (1997) Synergy trap: how companies lose the acquisition game. Simon & Schuster, New York, NY
Sirower ML (2003) Becoming a prepared acquirer. Eur Bus Forum 16:55–59
Villalonga B (2004) Diversification discount or premium? New evidence from the business tracking series. J Financ 42(2):943–963
Zaheer A, Castaner X, Souder R (2013) Synergy sources, target autonomy, and integration in acquisitions. J Manag 39(3):604–632
Zhou YM (2011) Synergy, coordination costs, and diversification choices. Strateg Manag J 32:624–639
Zollo M, Meier D (2008) What is M&A performance? Acad Manag Perspectives 22(3):55–77

Chapter 4
Synergy Management: From Pitfalls to Value

Abstract Integrating compatible elements of previous research with insights neglected by the strategic management, change management, organizational behavior and finance literature, this chapter advances a conceptual comprehensive framework to analyze synergy management in M&As. The framework highlights the main dimensions of synergy management, the most relevant synergy pitfalls and the ways to overcome them. An effective synergy management requires an analysis of five dimensions: the steps of the M&A process, the several values of synergy, the forbidding effects of poor synergy management, the potential causes of synergy inflation, and the selection of solutions to synergy pitfalls. The study changes the focus from a single, generic synergy trap to three more analytical, useful synergy pitfalls: the mirage, the gravity hill and the amnesia. By shedding light on synergy pitfalls, we enrich M&A literature and enhance practical solutions to reduce pitfalls in synergy management.

Keywords Mergers • Acquisition • Synergy • Pitfalls • Trap

4.1 The Synergy Pitfalls

The management of synergy is a relevant topic in M&As. The existence of several causes of synergy trap implies the existence of multiple types of risk. However, past studies reattach an unsuccessful synergy achievement to the risk of a "generic" trap. Research examining the severalpitfalls that may hinder the success of M&A deals remains surprisingly limited (Goold and Campbell 1998; Hitt et al. 2009). Since risks are reattached to a single and generic trap, managers and advisors have been given little guidance on the specific causes of "synergy pitfalls" and on the most effective way to avoid them.

Consequently, this gap requires the careful identification of the main types of synergy pitfalls by connecting each pitfall to the related cause and the most useful solutions (Fiorentino and Garzella 2015a, b). There are many pitfalls, and not a single trap, that could affect the synergy management that transforms a good M&A into a very bad deal (Hammond et al. 1998). The executives involved in M&A agreements have often underestimated the management of synergy pitfalls, and this lack of attention has substantially driven deal failure (Harding and Rovit 2005).

S. Garzella, R. Fiorentino, *Synergy Value and Strategic Management*,
Contributions to Management Science, DOI 10.1007/978-3-319-40671-8_4

Fig. 4.1 Improper synergy management

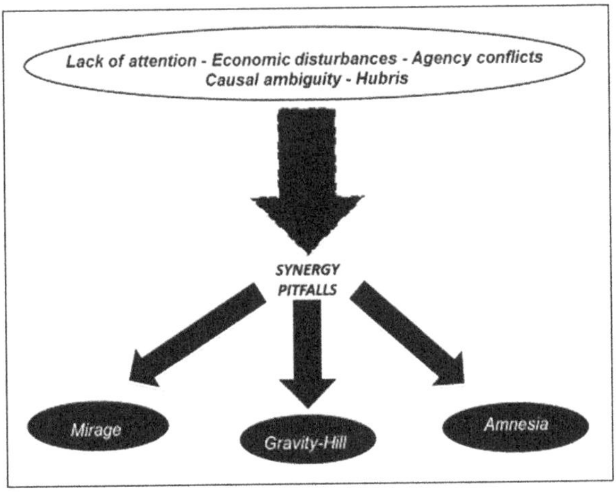

Despite significant progress, the extant synergy management literature still suffers from several shortcomings. There is a lack of integration across research paths pertinent to the study of synergy management.

We contribute to the existing literature by improving the analysis in the strategic management literature, considering and incorporating insights from new streams and the contiguous literature. Indeed, we answer to the call for further research about "how" to manage synergy pitfalls by developing a comprehensive framework that is useful for both scholars and practitioners.

We conceptualized three pitfalls about synergy assessment in the aim of building a bridge between theory and empirical evidences (Hammond et al. 1998). We named them the mirage, the gravity hill and the amnesia (Fig. 4.1).

4.1.1 The Mirage

The first common mistake is the "mirage of the synergies". As a real mirage, executives mislead themselves so much so that the expected deal is often connected to the difficulties of the actual circumstance and to the illusion of finding a remedy in external growth strategies (Goold and Campbell 1998). Executives, while unable to find sources of internal growth, seek, more or less unconsciously, the chance of synergy achievement by M&As as the only viable path to growth (Harding and Rovit 2005).

Box 4.1: The Case of Vivendi-Canal Plus-Seagram

For instance, Vivendi overestimated the synergic potential in the merger with Canal Plus and Seagram. Following the wave of mergers in the "media business", the achievable synergy expectations from the merger of the production, on the one hand, and the distribution of multimedia contents on traditional and new channels, on the other, worked for the senior executives of the French company as a "mirage" that later vanished during the integration (Harding and Rovit 2005).

Other times, the mirage of the synergies is artificially built by the management team, or a part of, on the basis of distorted informative processes, and in the aim of pursuing objectives which are not totally nor partly fit with the firms' goals (Haspeslagh and Jemison 1991). In these occasions, synergies are the means used by the management team in order to research for new stimuli and the replacement in different environments and businesses. In the worst scenario, they represent a way to dim the real financial statements or accountings (Porter 1987) (Fig. 4.2).

In the case of the mirage, therefore, the synergy value derives from assessment mistakes and it is different from the real value of the synergic potential.

4.1.2 The Gravity Hill

The second mistake is the "gravity hill" that induces to consider easy and close at hand circumstances that instead encompass elevated contents of strategic and organizational difficulties (Aaker 2001; Garzella 2006; Saint-Onge and Chatzkel 2009). Sometimes, managers involved in M&As tend to underestimate the difficulties to transform potential into effective synergies (Eccles et al. 1999). In these occasions this event follows a series of mistakes and carelessness that often rest on putting too much emphasis on the M&A arrangement (Haspeslagh and Jemison 1991). The M&A deals is generally thought of as a "finance move" rather than a "strategy move" and as a consequence senior executives pay no attention to the following integration.

As in front of a "gravity hill", the layout of the deal produces an optical illusion. The integration process, that is an uphill slope, appears as a very slight downhill. Thus synergy achievement, instead of quietly proceeding downhill, will risk coming back, more and more far from expected targets (Fig. 4.3).

The fact that M&As are generally preceded by the relief for the completion of the deal implies for the management "a misleading visual reference" or "an obstruction of the view of the horizon". This leads to the elimination of any correct reference, favoring a distorted perception of the integration "slope".

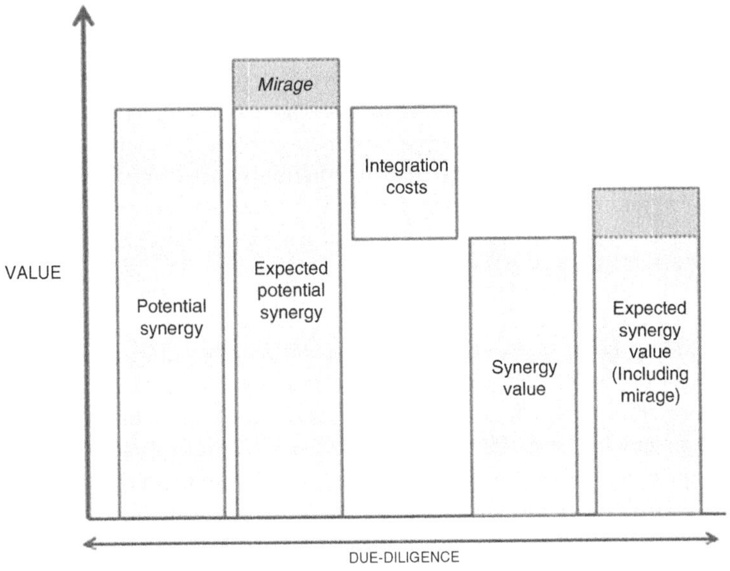

Fig. 4.2 The Mirage

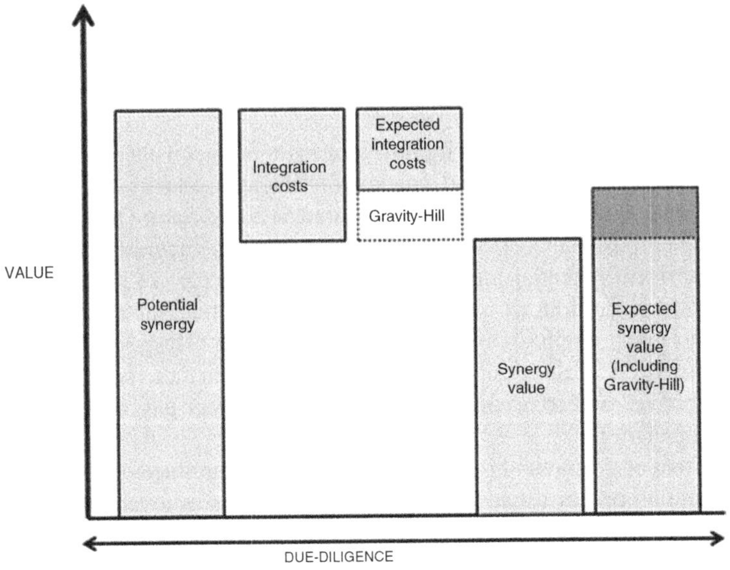

Fig. 4.3 The Gravity-Hill

Box 4.2: The Case of Columbia Pictures-Sony
The acquisition of Columbia Pictures from Sony is a good example of this mistake. The senior executives of the Japanese firm underestimated the difficulties hidden in the integration process of the American firm such as the state of the health of the "movie business", technological changes, and the cultural mismatch between the buyer and the target. A merger that look like a downhill represented, instead, a steep slope (Bruner 2004).

4.1.3 The Amnesia

A common situation in M&A deals is where there are the value of the synergic potential is high, real and well assessed, but the actions that are needed to transform synergy expectations in achieved synergies are not adequately implemented. As stricken by a sort of "amnesia", senior executives seem to forget those difficulties and considerations related to the transformation of the synergic potential into achieved synergies. Moreover, they often tend to overlook the opportunities identified during the due diligence. As a consequence the integration process through which achieved synergies are realized receives little attention and the deal is not sufficiently considered as a strategic challenge to be completed (Fig. 4.4).

In other words, senior executives seem to forget that the moment of the deal announcement is only the first step of a complex strategic process that must be followed by further steps such as the integration of the business and people and the reorganization of or the disinvestment from existing businesses when they cannot be properly integrated.

Box 4.3: The Case of Alitalia—KLM
For example, consider the failure of the post merger integration process between the Italian airline Alitalia and the Dutch KLM. After a deep and long due-diligence (lasted nearly 2 years) and a "cohabitation" period (a year and a half with a full operating joint-venture), the marriage broke down. During the due-diligence, the high synergic potential was properly assessed. Following a difficult turnaround, Alitalia was in good control of a large domestic market, but it also had limited financial resources and a fleet unsuitable for long-haul flights. Vice versa, KLM had no domestic market, but high trade and tariff capacity and an efficient traffic network to benefit from intercontinental flights via the hub in Amsterdam. The potential difficulties in integration, caused by large differences in cultures and leadership styles, emerged and were carefully analyzed. However, a striking amnesia about the actions relative to the execution of the integration of business and people led to the stop of the merger process.

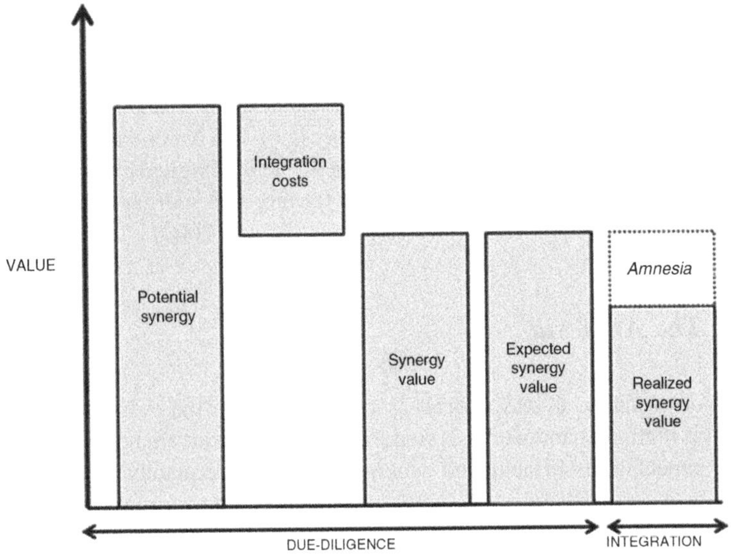

Fig. 4.4 The Amnesia

Although we presented a separate description of each mistake, they can potentially occur together in the same M&A process for example when synergy expectations are ambiguous, the integration process harder than expected, and companies forget to implement the required actions.

Box 4.4: The Case of General Motors—Fiat

The deal signed between Fiat Group and General Motors in 2000 is illustrative. General Motors and the Fiat Group developed an M&A through an equity-based agreement based on a stock exchange: the 20 % of Fiat Group versus the 6 % of General Motors. Operating synergies in Europe and South America were the primary motive for the M&A. Consequently, the merging firms realized two joint ventures: Fiat-GM Powertrain, related to the production activities of engines and transmissions; and GM-Fiat Worldwide Purchasing, related to supply-chain activities. The real synergistic value was most likely lower than the assessed synergy because the operating activities involved in the agreement were limited. However, the deal provided strategic rigidity in the product strategies of both firms. The difficulties in the integration process, based on cultural differences, were much larger than expected. Moreover, the deal also failed because the senior executives of the involved firms forgot to implement some of the strategic and operating actions provided in the opening agreement.

4.2 The Management of Synergy Pitfalls

Identifying synergy pitfalls is certainly important. However, it risk meaning an useless exercise without a careful examination of what can be done to avoid or limit them.

Since it is useful to verify the existence of potential synergy, the synergy management may start from the pre-deal steps. Since the sources of potential synergy are based on either strategy or finance, the synergy assessment should analytically identify several values of synergy. Indeed, some synergy pitfalls might hide behind extra-synergy motives.

Moreover, since the achievement of expected synergies is generally difficult, firms should estimate the difficulties and the integration costs in the pre-deal steps. The integration approach, according to the assessment of potential synergy and organizational difficulties, may be developed prior to concluding the deal. The assessment of difficulties may analyze many of the issues highlighted in the various literature streams. Moreover, the distinction between revenue growth and cost-saving synergies should be useful in the assessment process to identify potential difficulties at the integration stage. Consequently, the literature suggests the importance of the integration step. Furthermore, a lack of attention to organizational issues should be the cause of some other pitfalls. This issue imply adding organization fit to the strategic fit analysis (Stahl et al. 2013).

To develop a framework for managing synergy, we propose that the synergy pitfalls literature can be significantly enriched and its power enhanced by incorporating insights from organizational behavior and finance and by further elaborating on the implications of the literature streams to avoid synergy pitfalls. Consistently, the management of synergy pitfalls should embrace five main dimensions: the management of synergy in the main step of the M&A process; the analysis of the several values of synergy; the recognition of the forbidding effects of inappropriate synergy management; the evaluation of the potential causes of improper synergy management; and the selection of the most relevant solutions to synergy pitfalls.

4.2.1 The Management of Synergy in the Main Step of the M&A Process

Synergy management plays a key role in mergers and acquisitions (M&A). First, it plays a key role in the decision-making process; and second, it plays a key role at the integration stage. Studies of due diligence are generally focused on assessment and measurement issues (Colombo et al. 2007), whereas research about integration is primarily based on organizational issues (Vaara 2003). Synergy studies must integrate results from the due-diligence and integration research.

At due-diligence stage it is fundamental to consider the risks of a bad synergy valuation (Haspeslagh and Jemison 1991; Rappaport and Sirower 1999): synergies should be definitively contextualized, accurately forecasted, and appropriately discounted with reference to their probability and timing (Evans and Bishop 2001). In any event, what happens at the integration stage is also relevant to synergy management (Sales and Mirvis 1984; Buono and Bowditch 1989). The potential synergy is not automatically realized and that the extent of synergy realization depends on the actions effectively adopted after the "closing date" (Datta 1991; Hunt 1990; Schweiger et al. 1987). The studies' findings suggest that considerable interaction and coordination are necessary to exploit the synergy that may be present between firms engaged in a merger or acquisition (Birkinshaw et al. 2000; Haspeslagh and Jemison 1991; Laarson 1990; Pablo 1994; Shrivastava 1986).

4.2.2 An Analysis of the Several Values of Synergy

The management of synergy pitfalls should consider: synergy expectations, synergy realizations and the integration costs to realize potential synergy. The aim is to improve the realized synergy value resulting from the difference between the potential synergy and the integration costs.

The prior synergy values should be further analyzed with respect to additional perspectives: from a side, with respect to the nature of the synergy by distinguishing operating, financial and tax synergies (Garzella and Fiorentino 2014); from another side, with respect to the issues of "cost savings" and "revenue enhancements" (Devos et al. 2009; Kaplan et al. 2000; Andrade et al. 2001). Furthermore, it would be useful to assess the organizational level at which several values of synergies are allocated (Kroll and Caples 1987).

4.2.3 The Recognition of the Forbidding Effects of an Improper Approach to Synergy Management

Consistent with the synergy values, the effects of poor synergy management should be related to the gaps among potential synergy, expected synergy and realized synergy.

The overestimation of potential synergy is a source of poor management at the due diligence stage (Haspeslagh and Jemison 1991; Seyhun 1990; Sirower 1997). This error results in an assessment of expected synergy higher than the real synergy value. Consequently, firms are expected to choose a partner that is not the best, whether the choice is made deliberately or involuntarily.

Moreover, the misassessment of integration costs is another potential effect of poor management. This approach pursue to consider the expectation of integration costs, in the pre deal step, lower than the real integration costs as a potential effect of an improper synergy management. The risk is that the integration process will result more difficulty than expected.

Finally, high potential acquisitions are often the most challenging because they require effective interaction and coordination to realize their potential (Larsson and Finkelstein 1999; Lubatkin and O'Neill 1987). Since the existence of synergy value is not a guarantee for synergy value realization, the final effect of poor synergy management can be a realized synergy value that is lower than the synergy value (Barkema and Schijven 2008; Pablo 1994; Zollo and Singh 2004).

4.2.4 The Evaluation of the Potential Causes of Improper Synergy Management

The reasons underlying ineffective synergy assessment and realization can vary. The theoretical foundations of these causes can be viewed as follows: the bounded rationality and the attention based views; agency theory and information asymmetry; Gort's theory and economic disturbances; the resource based view and the "causal ambiguity" concept; and the market efficiency theory and the "hubris hypothesis". These causes are not mutually exclusive, but each one provides a perspective that is complementary to the others in an unified view.

The firms should carefully analyze them to exclude the existence, or detect its presence by adopting the most appropriate countermoves.

4.2.5 The Selection of Potential Solutions to Poor Synergy Management

The M&A literature provides some generic suggestions useful in managing deals. These solutions are generally reattached to M&A management rather than to synergy management. Moreover, solutions are typically linked to a single trap instead of to specific pitfalls. Consequently the challenge is, on the one hand, to identify the right tools, behaviors and actions with reference to the most relevant pitfall and, on the other hand, to develop a systematic road map to avoid pitfalls, although each solution to one pitfall may have positive effects on others.

The challenge is using the right guidelines to manage each synergy pitfalls in the several M&As (Fig. 4.5).

By integrating these five dimensions, firms should have an effective framework for synergy management pitfalls in M&As. Each dimension contributes to answering a specific question that decision makers must analyze to avoid or limit pitfalls.

The analysis of M&A steps answers the question of "when" the pitfalls should embrace synergy management. Both the due diligence and the integration stages have hidden pitfalls. An examination of synergy values answers the question of

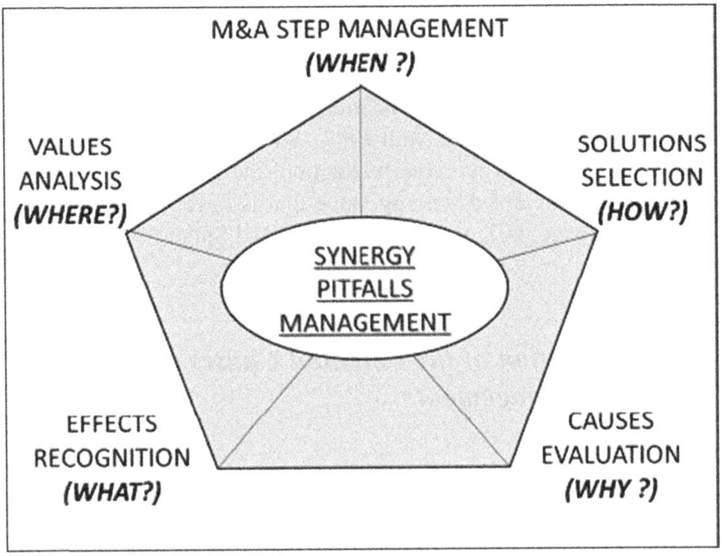

Fig. 4.5 A framework for synergy pitfalls management

"where" pitfalls may occur: in the assessment of potential synergy, in the analysis of integration costs or in the achievement of realized synergy. The investigation into fearful effects answers the question of "what" consequences can progress to a value of "realized synergy" lower than that of "expected synergy". The effects of unsuccessful synergy assessment and realization in M&A may be the overestimation of potential synergy, the underestimation of the difficulties in transforming potential into realized synergy, and the underestimation of the need for synergy integration. The check of possible causes answers the question of "why" pitfalls may occur: agency conflicts, economic disturbances, causal ambiguity, hubris, or lack of attention. Tools, behaviors and actions, combined in the advanced framework, suggest "how" overcome synergy pitfalls.

In the strategic planning stage, the framework suggests the most important dimensions to analyze, requiring management to be aware of potential synergy pitfalls. Managers should analyze each M&A option according to the five questions (when, where, what, why and how) and identify possible answers among the various alternatives suggested. In this way, managers can select the partner with high potential synergy and provide an effective assessment of synergy value in the due-diligence step. In the integration stage, executives should achieve the full potential synergy. The framework represents a simple but important diagnostic model for synergy pitfalls and, if required, allows for the activation of correctives.

4.3 How to Overcome Synergy Pitfalls: Tools and Actions

In this section we introduce some tools, behaviors and actions that overcome such a challenge. Each solution may overcome a pitfall and at the same time may have positive effects on the others. The challenge in M&As is to find the best way to manage these tools so to adopt the best behaviors and actions.

By merging the insights from several synergy management literature streams, these solutions should be systematized based on three guidelines: selection of the merging firm to find M&As where potential synergies exist; synergy measurement to effectively measure potential synergy and integration costs; and management of the integration process to completely realize the expected synergy value.

Target selection is a relevant topic in M&A processes (Capron and Shen 2007; Shimuzu et al. 2004), although target selection is much more studied in the context of strategic alliances (Cummings and Holmberg 2012; Hitt et al. 2000).

Analysis of distinctive resources and partner selection is associated with the managerial competence necessary for the synergistic combination of organizational structures and operations. Indeed, the key determinants of synergy value creation are the "strategic fit" and the "organizational fit" (King et al. 2004; Weber 2011). However, analysis of those fits is very difficult because it must quantify "soft" variables that are difficult to measure, such as skills or cultural values. Firms may assess synergy based on the target's business strategies, corporate strategies, potential resource exploration and exploitation (Ahuja and Katila 2001; Capron and Pistre 2002). However, the organizational side is also relevant because mergers generally lead to changes in governance, leadership style and human resources. However, organizational compatibility can occur both for similarities and for non-compliance (Hayward 2002; Tanriverdi and Venkatraman 2005). Sometimes, organizational compatibility can promote organizational dynamics by exploiting the similarity and the similarity of the firms' values, ideals and styles of government. At other times, benefits arise out of the possibility of combining organizational structures so that they complement each other, thus limiting gaps and areas of weakness in governance and management processes. Furthermore, the operations level is as important as strategic and organizational issues. "Operations fit" should be more clearly oriented towards complementarity because firms should avoid the risk of an excess of similar resources and there is often a need to dispose of underutilized assets (Shelton 1988; Zott and Amit 2010). The selection of a firm with which to merge should be oriented toward strategic alignment, organizational compatibility and operations complementarity (Fig. 4.6).

In order to analyze and realize these aims, firms need useful synergy measurement models. Because synergy value is the present value of the expected synergy flows deriving from a deal, discounted back at a rate that reflects the riskiness of those flows, these measurement models should assess the value of potential synergy depending on the financial flows related to the potential M&A synergies, on their temporal distribution, and on the discount rate (Rappaport 1986; Demirakos et al. 2004; Damodaran 2005). M&As can deliver synergies through increased revenues, cost savings, risk reduction and an abatement of financial needs.

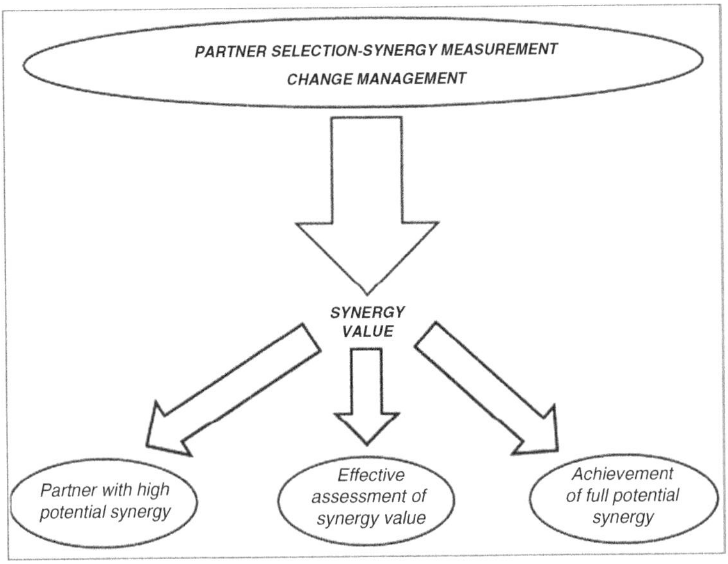

Fig. 4.6 Effective synergy management

Consequently, studies have suggested that valuations may be based on prior partner selection, which requires forecasting post-merger cash flows according to the planned post-merger strategy (Cullinan et al. 2004). This process implies the grant of autonomous importance to forecasting synergy forms that represent the analytical dimensions of strategy and organizational structures (Gupta and Gerchak 2002). Firms should forecast the synergistic nature distinguishing operating synergies from financial and tax synergies; the financial exhibition of synergistic flows, higher revenues or lower costs; and the organizational allocation of synergies at one SBU, at one division or at the corporate level (Garzella and Fiorentino 2014).

Based on organizational behavior and change management studies, firms should develop effective integration processes at the pre-deal stage. The goal of the integration process is the full achievement of expected synergy by the management of change inertia, the overcoming of cultural differences, and the attention to pondering HR relevance (Buono and Bowditch 1989; Datta 1991; David and Singh 1994; Hambrick and Cannella 1993; Schuler and Jackson 2001). To pursue this aim, and based on the findings of the analysis of M&A features, firms should first choose the right integration approach and second adopt all of the planned actions. Because uncertainties and ambiguities generally surround integration issues, firms should pay attention to the implementation of planned actions and eventually change along the way (Vaara 2003). Moreover, the role of decision makers is critical for the success of the integration process (Haspeslagh and Jemison 1991; Vaara 2002).

Based on the prior selection guidelines and consistently with the proposed pitfalls, we can advance a matrix that points up three main ways to overcame each trap (Fig. 4.7).

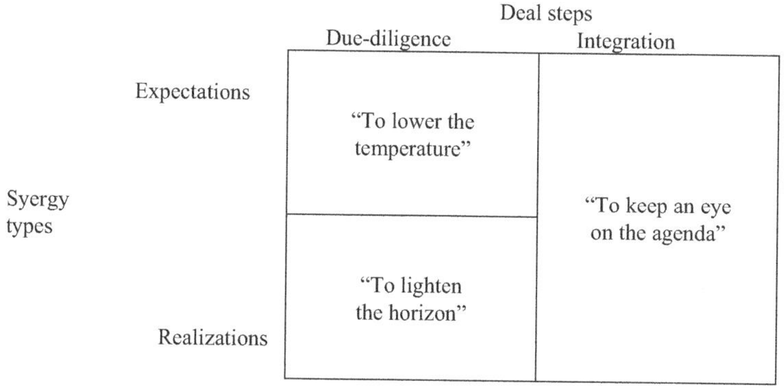

Fig. 4.7 Ways to overcome synergy pitfalls

Identifying synergy pitfalls is certainly important yet it risks being an useless exercise without a careful examination of what can be done to avoid or limit them. In this session we introduce some tools, behaviors and actions that, combined with the advanced framework, suggest "how" overcome pitfalls in synergy management. Solutions, advanced with reference to each pitfall, may avoid or limit a hidden dangers and, at the same time, may have positive effects on the others. The challenge in M&As is to find the best way to manage these tools so to adopt the best behaviors and actions.

4.3.1 Avoiding the Mirage: Let's Reduce the Temperature

In order to avoid or limit the risks of synergy overestimation, managers should "reduce the temperature", promoting a more effective assessment of external growth strategies. They should understand whether the deal is only the answer to the frenzy due to actual difficulties or external pressure and distinguish real synergy from traps (Table 4.1).

4.3.1.1 Pay Careful Attention to Advisory Agreement

Since in the assessment process a key role is played by advisors and consulting firms, merging companies may pay attention to the drafting process of the professional agreement (McLaughlin 1992). A misevaluation of synergies could be a result of the influence of advisor analysis (Russo and Perrini 2006). When the payment of the advisors, involved in synergy assessment, is linked to the deal value, their analysis could be deliberately high to maximize their fees. Signing advisor agreement where the payment is linked to realized synergy rather than the deal value may avoid or limit synergy overestimation.

Table 4.1 How to avoid or limit the mirage

Mirage	
When?	Due diligence
Where?	Potential synergy
What?	Overestimation of synergy value
Why?	– Distortive information processes – Agency conflicts – High level of competition – Ineffective assessment models – Hubris – Inter-firm causal ambiguity
How?	– Pay careful attention to the advisory agreement – Verify the alignment between one's strategy and the deal – Conduct a careful analysis of the reasons for an M&A – Assess the "expected synergy " carefully – Use a risk-management approach for board-level discussion – Leverage the acquisition experience

4.3.1.2 Conduct a Careful Analysis of the Reasons for An M&A

The careful analysis of M&A reasons could lighten the firms' strategic horizon. First, the meditation on specific reasons of the deal, instead of a generic synergy, may push managers to link each motive with expected synergy (Berkovitch and Narayanan 1993; Cartwright and Schoenberg 2006; Goold and Campbell 2000; Mukherjee et al. 2004). Accordingly, motives should not be generic nor ambiguous. Second, the identified motives indicate the directions for the integration and in this way they may prevent possible synergy illusions.

4.3.1.3 Verify the Alignment Between One's Strategy and the Deal

Since M&As are often driven by extra-synergy reasons, firms should verify the alignment between their own strategies and the deal. Managers should instead carefully check the deal's alignment to corporate and business strategy (Allred et al. 2005; Porter 1987). This means a verification of the weight of operating synergy and their alignment to future strategies. Financial analysis may be positioned in the context of an overarching aim and intent. If the motives underlying a combination are concerning the managerial illusions more than the company's strategic aim and intent, a successful combination is unlikely to occur since there are no real synergies to reach.

4.3.1.4 Assess the "Expected Synergy" Carefully

Synergy value depends on the forecasting of potential synergy. From this perspective, factors that influence the forecasting of synergy expectations may be identified in: synergy form, synergy timing and the likelihood of achievement (Accenture 2007; Damodaran 2005; Devos et al. 2009; Fiorentino and Garzella 2015a; Garzella and Fiorentino 2014; Houston et al. 2001). Each element needs a careful analysis in order to avoid the mirage. Accordingly, to support an effective assessment of synergy value, firms may develop a "synergy statement" able to give representation, in terms of financial flows related to potential synergies. Firms, advisors and consultants should try to understand where synergies arise, either at the SBU or Corporate level; how much the potential synergy is; and what the specific items of synergy are.

4.3.1.5 Use a Risk-Management Approach For Board-Level Discussion

Since different types of synergy have different likelihood of achievement, firms should use risk-management approach for board level discussion. In fact, several discount rate are needed to estimate synergy value. In this regard, Sirower and Sahni (2006) propose the use of the SVAR, a tool for assessing the relative magnitude of synergy risk. Two perspectives could drive the analysis. On the one hand, revenue of the synergy appear riskier than their cost. On the other, operating synergy is riskier than financial and tax synergy.

4.3.1.6 Leverage the Acquisition Experience

The adoption of prior suggested solutions should be improved by leveraging the acquisition experience. Since a positive relation exists between acquisition experience and the success of M&A (Barkema et al. 1996; Haleblian and Finkelstein 1999), firms should try to leverage their own experience in the synergy assessment. It implies that, where firms have prior experience in M&As, feedbacks from recent deals should be deliberately used in the due-diligence stage. Instead, when firms have poor experience in M&As, they could appeal to external experience: by learning from executives involved in M&AS in the past (Haunschild and Beckmann 1998); by learning from the evaluation of similar deals in the same industry or context (Haunschild and Miner 1997); by involving consulting firms and advisors specialized in M&As (Damodaran 2005).

4.3.2 Avoiding the Gravity-Hill: Let's Lighten the Horizon

In order to reduce the risks of integration cost's underestimation, managers should "lighten the horizon" to sight possible climbs. Having clear aims and strategic guidelines favors the right perception of potential synergy and integration difficulties (Table 4.2).

Table 4.2 How to avoid or limit the Gravity-Hill

Gravity-Hill	
When?	Due diligence
Where?	Integration costs
What?	Overestimation of synergy value
Why?	– Inappropriate background of the management involved – Secrecy – Speed – Overconfidence – Lack of attention – High costs of coordination
How	– Give more relevance to the audit committee – Obtain M&A insurance – Establish a termination fee – Carefully assess the "integration costs" – Build cross-functional teams from technical, operational and financial positions – Establish a courtship period before the marriage

4.3.2.1 Give More Relevance to the Audit Committee

Indeed, greater involvement of the audit committee may help to highlight future criticalities, integration costs and unclear motives behind an M&A deal (Gates 2006; Nadler 2004; Zhang et al. 2007). The controls of audit committee members may concern not only accounting and procedural elements but also financial and strategic factors related to the M&A. The audit committee could play the role of the 'talking cricket', suggesting points as need of a deeper analysis and integration costs requiring a more careful assessment. In this respect, the audit committee may be actively involved in the due-diligence process, as well as in the integration step.

4.3.2.2 Obtain M&A Insurance

If you are not a serial acquirers and you have not developed a successful experience in integration processes, you may obtain M&A insurance or set up a termination fee. M&A insurance may reduce the effects of a gravity-hill (Galpin and Herndon 2000; Martinius 2005). Firms may be able to acquire M&A insurance that may provide protection from hidden costs by a thorough due diligence step. Advisors and consultants generally offer a risk and insurance due diligence exercise on target acquisitions to augment and supplement the acquirer's assessment. By identifying potential areas of exposure, insurance help firms plan for future contingencies.

4.3.2.3 Establish a Termination Fee

A termination fee that represents a relatively recent instrument for protecting the deal (André et al. 2007; Officer 2003). To have a way out, termination fee provisions require the payment of a certain amount in case of a breakdown of the deal (Bates and Lemmon 2003). By doing so, firms facing possible synergy pitfalls can avoid the negative consequences of an early termination of the deal through this fee payment.

4.3.2.4 Carefully Assess the "Integration Costs"

Since the achievement of expected synergy is not automatic, firms may carefully assess the costs related to integration and coordination problems that should arise after the merger (Capron et al. 1998; Hill et al. 1992; Zhou 2011). The managers involved in the deal could ask the costs needed to realize each type of expected synergy emerging from a "synergy statement". By this way they should give representation, in terms of financial flows, to integration costs. As for potential synergy they should try to understand where costs arise and how much they are.

4.3.2.5 Build Cross-Functional Teams from Technical, Operational and Financial Positions

A key role should have building cross functional teams from technical, operational and financial positions. The involvement of managers from different areas and from different levels may improve the effectiveness of the due diligence process and can help identifying the main areas of coordination for post-merger integration (Cartwright and Schoenberg 2006; Damodaran 2005). Members of the buy team generally come from financial position or background. They have a "financial" mindset and their assessment about synergies were mostly informed by financial models and ratios. They often did not know very much about manufacturing, marketing and business. Each area can pose a different obstacle or an innovative solution previously ignored by other areas. Changing the point of view you can avoid falling into an optical illusion.

4.3.2.6 Establish a Courtship Period Before the Marriage

Anyway, the potential difficulties may clearly arise from testing a courtship period before the marriage. When the potential difficulties and integration costs should be very high, the merging firms may experience a time to know better each other (Uhlenbruck et al. 2006). The engagement between firms should range along the main forms of alliance agreement (Colombo et al. 2007). This period can reduce problems of information asymmetry and to understand potential tensions and cultural problems. The establishment of prior interactions can favor trust and action planning. Courtship may lead to reduce potential post marriage difficulties.

Table 4.3 How to avoid or limit the amnesia

Amnesia	
When?	Integration
Where?	Realized synergy
What?	Failure to achieve synergy value
Why?	– Absence of plans to deliver synergies – Intra-firm causal ambiguity – Lack of attention – Change of inertia – Cultural differences – Retention of top management
How?	– Pay attention to the action plan – Adopt a "project oriented approach" for control processes – Indicate a transition team – Carefully analyze and organize the cultural integration – Create a "burning platform" – Select the correct integration approach

4.3.3 *Avoiding the Amnesia: Let's Keep an Eye on the Agenda*

For mitigating the likelihood of a lack of attention in integration, you should "keep an eye on the agenda" so to maintain the milestones of synergy realization under control. Assigning clear responsibility over the steps and timing needed for synergy realization, firms may also reduce the risks of integration forgetfulness (Table 4.3).

4.3.3.1 Pay Attention to the Action Plan

Drawing up a well designed action plan, defining milestones, timing and the likelihood of achievement at each step is critical to capture the forecasted synergies (Devos et al. 2009; Kpmg 1999). Firms do not have plans for delivering synergies and no one is generally responsible for them. As a consequence, synergy achievement becomes increasingly difficult over time, affecting speed and costs of the integration (Bert et al. 2003; Colombo et al. 2007: 215; Haspeslagh and Jemison 1991; Ancona et al. 2001). This approach may be put into practice by dividing the whole process into milestones, interrelated "blocks" which specify the period and the expected date of realization of each type and sub-type of synergy. The attention to the main integration stages can help reduce intrafirm ambiguity associated with the complexity and temporal distance of the M&A process.

4.3.3.2 Carefully Analyze and Organize the Cultural Integration

Anyway, the successful achievement of synergy is affected by human and cultural factors underlying the relationships among managers of different companies (Cartwright and Cooper 1996; Nahavandi and Malekzadeh 1988; Vaara 2003). This factors are very relevant, specially in the integration step, when mixing values, know-how and competences of the manager of both companies could put at risk the realized synergy value (Chatterjee 1992; Datta 1991). The risks of delay, resistances and integration's failure is very high without a collaborative approach.

4.3.3.3 Adopt a "Project-Oriented Approach" For Control Processes

The need for correct and rapid achievement of expected synergy highlights the opportunities for firms to have a project-oriented approach (Lorange and Vancil 1977; Goold and Quinn 1990) for control processes which may facilitate the success (Cording et al. 2008). To respect expectations in terms of timing, the control process requires a careful monitoring of any over-optimistic expectations, of any unforeseen problems that could arise during the integration, and of the lack of managerial attention towards the actions. The setting and the identification of intermediate goals as organizational milestones is a mechanism that can reduce risks of amnesia. The adoption of a project-based approach ensure the effective monitoring of integration process, so as to render possible the revision, improvement and innovation, stage by stage, the work required and necessary for the achievement of synergy.

4.3.3.4 Indicate a Transition Team

This approach should be better supported by indicating a transition team. Without the involvement of the management there are many risks of amnesia, turning a good deal in a failure M&A due to the inconsistency of the communication of strategic intent and actions to be implemented (Vaara 2003). One of the tools that companies have recently turned to speed up the process of integration is the creation of "transition teams" that have the aim of rescuing the firms toward the "stable period" (Marks and Mirvis 2000). These teams may involve also "experts of M&A" that have managed people's reactions to the integration in several occasions and in different contexts Haleblian and Finkelstein 1999; Zollo and Singh 2004). It is advisable to clearly define the roles distinguishing figures or functions that are "change makers" from those who are "agents of change" (Hitt et al. 2009). The change makers promote the integration through behavior, styles, actions and attitudes consistent with the M&A. The change agents are identified in managers who are entrusted with the role of planning, support and implementation of the integration tools.

4.3.3.5 Create a "Burning Platform"

The leaders of change, may create a "burning platform". In the absence of careful design of the change management process, firms are not able to achieve expected synergy. The response of human resources to synergy achievement depends largely on the willingness to support the integration process and the management's ability to convey the reasons for the need for change (Buono and Bowditch 1989; Duck 1993; Kotter 1995). Managers may create the "burning platform". The metaphor of the burning platform is born from the example of a man who dives into the icy sea as an oil rig in flames and well represents the need to abandon the current state to face a difficult situation, but although still better (Schweizer and Patzelt 2012). The motivation to realize the expected synergy must be forcefully brought to the surface in a participatory manner: everyone may acquire a full understanding of the need for M&A. The awareness of the inevitability of the integration should be the prerequisite for sound management of the process.

4.3.3.6 Select the Correct Integration Approach

For these reasons it is useful to select the right integration approach. Since there are different types of acquisitions, studies suggest several integration approaches that firms can adopt (Cartwright and Cooper 1993; Haspeslagh and Jemison 1991; Teerikangas and Very 2006; Vaara 2003). The challenge is to select the right integration approach based on the features of the different kinds of M&As. The analysis of M&A types and the following development of the right integration approach should push executives to avoid lapse in concentration about the synergy achievement.

4.4 The Synergy Statement

The determination of the synergy value presupposes awareness and comprehension of what are the fundamental assumptions and the key variables about the growth strategies of involved firms. The validity of the strategic analysis, the understanding of what are the main success factors of the integration process, the awareness of the strengths and weaknesses of companies are the inevitable premise of a good quantitative analysis of synergy. Since firms should use all of the tools that are useful to facilitate the passage from the qualitative analyses to those that are "value based", synergy assessment cannot be separated from value estimation by articulating the connection between the strategic analysis and the valuation models.

The potential synergies should be translated into financial forecasts identifying the changes that the deal will produce on the cash flows of the companies involved (Rappaport 1986). To pursue this aim, we propose a synergy statement based on a multi-level chart that implies an in-depth analysis of each type and sub-type of synergy.

Of course, the proposed synergy statement is an illustrative example and the accuracy of the analysis and the number of items are indeed dependent on the context and on the specific M&A.

This tool, using a multidimensional chart, may help researchers and practitioners to understand what are the specific synergistic flows related to each type of synergy and what is the overall amount of synergy in a defined period of the integration process.

Besides leading to the measurement of the synergy value, the synergy statement forces the management to analyse the main dimensions of synergies. In this way the synergy statement reduces the risk of typical estimation errors and synergy trap (Sirower 1997). This tool highlights the strategic factors—type, size, timing and likelihood of realization—developed and tested in the model.

Since various types of synergy differently affect the value of synergy, three categorizations are especially relevant about the synergy form: the nature of synergy, the financial exhibition of synergistic flows, and the organizational level of synergy allocation (Table 4.4).

Table 4.4 The synergy statement

	SBU 1	SBU ...	SBU n	Corporate	Total synergies
Revenues					
Advertising costs					
Delivery costs					
Costs of traders					
Other trade costs					
Market synergies					
Production costs					
Human resources costs (production)					
External production costs					
Other production costs					
Raw material costs					
Raw material inventory variation					
Depreciation costs					
Product inventory variation					
Immobilisation variation					
Manufacturing and supply chain synergies					
Research and development costs					
Headquarters office costs					
Other infrastructural costs					
Infrastructural and headquarters synergies					
Financial needs					
Interest rate					
Financial synergies					
Tax burden					
Tax synergies					
Total synergies					

To support the analysis, the lines of the synergy statement propose the categorization of synergistic flows: by nature, in operating, financial and tax synergies; by financial exhibition, in revenues and costs. Indeed, following the need of sub-categorizations, operating synergies are distinguished among "market synergies", "manufacturing and supply chain synergies", and "infrastructural and headquarters synergies". A pure operating logic aiming to increase market power and the efficiency of manufacturing processes is the basis of operating synergies (Sirower 1997) (Fig. 4.8).

Operating synergies can be linked to the existence of activities in the value chain of the involved firms and are based on sharing resources and processes (e.g. sales networks, manufacturing plants, research laboratories, materials, etc.). These synergies can change the conditions of the profitability of a company if: the commonality of activities allows to share expenses and structural factors, or push to the growth of the cumulative volume of operational activities of the same type, resulting in cost savings based on economies of scale, on a more intense exploitation of the available operational capabilities (manufacturing, logistics, research & development, procurement, etc.); as a result of scope economies, deriving from the increased accumulation of skills, and the characters of uniqueness/superiority of the products, they ensure higher revenues; they reduce the incidence of diversification costs because of their distribution on a larger number of products. Indeed, operating

M&A INTEGRATION LOGICS

Portfolio Logic (investment reduction)
↳ diversifiable risk reduction

Financial resources sharing logic
↳ financial loans reduction
↳ financing rates reduction
↳ → → financing costs reduction

Tax benefits exploitation logic
↳ taxable income reduction
↳ tax band reduction
↳ → → income tax reduction

Resource/capabilities/skills sharing/transfer logic
↳ operating costs (total or unitary) reduction
↳ price increase
↳ sales increase
↳ → → revenues/margins increase

Fig. 4.8 M&A integration logics

synergies should be related to the ability to use the same skills and knowledge (marketing, technical, scientific, logistic, administrative, etc.) through the transfer of distinctive capabilities and exclusive powers, from one company to another, allowing to boost and complement the technical and managerial know-how (Goold and Campbell 1998) (Fig. 4.9).

Thus, it may be useful to distinguish synergies related to the market from those related to manufacturing and supply processes. By sharing resources, processes, and customers, M&A deals aim to increase, on the revenue enhancement side, volumes and prices of products and, on the cost savings side, to optimise volumes and unitary costs of inputs. The source of market synergies is the possibility to serve the same customers with several products that complement one another to increase overall profitability. Integrative actions may aim to obtain both outcomes at the same time by exploiting synergies of customer perception, sales network, or advertising. Manufacturing synergies arise from the possibility to produce or use the same components and the possibility to optimise the supply chain or IT systems.

In particular, firms may achieve synergies in the supply chain by centralising purchases and achieving better input quality, timing and cost. Similarly, firms may develop infrastructural and headquarters synergies by jointly managing common support activities, such as human resources management.

Financial synergies are created to reduce financing needs and costs by sharing financial resources and exploiting possible cash flow asynchronies between involved firms (Porter Liebeskind 2000). The financial synergies can be achieved primarily by reducing the risk level, decreasing the cost of debt capital, limiting the total amount of funding, increasing lending capacity, and improving knowledge of financial markets. In this way, firms may reduce their global financial needs and their costs. For example, an important component of financial synergies is the possibility to reduce the risk of diversification by applying logic based on the creation of a corporate portfolio. However, this logic is not sustainable as a strategic driver in manufacturing firms because financial firms, such as investment funds, will always be more efficient and effective in exploiting diversification strategies (Mathur and Kenyon 1998).

The final sub-category consists of tax synergies that aim to decrease taxation pressures on firms (Copeland 1994) by reducing the taxable income and the tax band.

Furthermore, the columns of the tool highlights the organizational level of synergy allocation. In this way, we should observe and measure synergy in each SBU and at the corporate level.

The size of synergy is then described in details, since executives should place the values of the various synergies in specific cells of the table, thus promoting the correct estimation of the size of each type of synergies and the assessment of the total synergistic flow.

The synergy statement considers also the timing since the reference period for the total implementation of the synergies can be usefully and reasonably distinguished in intermediate periods (not necessarily corresponding to the calendar year

TANGIBLE OPERATING SYNERGIES
(Resource/capabilities/customers sharing)

Market: sharing of customers exhange/communication activities/resources
- *Commercial network*
- *Physical distribution*
- *Advertising*
- *Order management*
- *After sales services*

Manufacturing: manufacturing activities/resources sharing
- *Common production phases*
- *Inbound Logistics*
- *Components manufacturing*
- *Maintenance*

Procurement: input sharing
- *Centralized purchasing*

Technologies: activities/resources sharing for new technologies development
- *Unification of research centers*

Infrastructural: support activities/resources sharing
- *Information and accounting systems unification*
- *Centralized human resource management*
- *Centralized legal issues management*

INTANGIBLES OPERATING SYNERGIES
(Capabilties/knowledge/competencies sharing/transfer)
- *Technologies transfer*
- *Managerial capabilities transfer*
- *Managerial know-how transfer*

FINANCIAL SYNERGIES
(Earnings/Cash flows complementary trends)
- *Self-financing at group level*
- *Investments reduction*
- *Financing costs differences among SBUs*
- *Operating improvement in financial market*

TAX SYNERGIES
(taxable income compensation/transfer)
- *Offset losses*
- *Existence of favorable tax regimes*
- *Taxable income compensation/transfer opportunities*

Fig. 4.9 Synergy check-list

or a quarter). As a consequence, in order to improve the analysis and the measurement of synergies, it should be useful to develop a synergy statement for each step of the implementation process. In this way, the specific synergistic flows are allocated over time to the year/period in which the integration process is structured and the synergies will be realized. The assessment of the timing of the synergy is very relevant since it affects the discount rate and the synergy value.

The measurement process is completed by the consideration of the likelihood of realization since it affects the measurement process by its rationalization in the assessment of the discount rates of the synergistic flows of each synergy statement (Cullinan et al. 2004). The synergy value will be achieved through the actualization of the results arising from the various synergy statements of the interim periods. It's possible—based on the complexity of the deal, the information needs and data availability- to use more than one rate in the discounting process in order to reflect the different likelihood of realization of each type and timing of synergy.

This tool shows its strength in the assessment of synergies at the corporate level, such as when it is necessary to measure synergy expectations in M&A situations to value them (Porter 1980).

References

Aaker D (2001) Strategic market management. Wiley, New York, NY

Accenture (2007) Strategy in action. The synergy enigma. http://www.accenture.com

Ahuja G, Katila A (2001) Technological acquisition and the innovation performance of acquiring firms: a longitudinal study. Strateg Manag J 22(3):197–220

Allred BB, Boal KB, Holstein WK (2005) Corporations as stepfamilies: a new metaphor for explaining the fate of merged and acquired companies. Acad Manag Exec 19(3):23–37

Ancona DG, Okhuysen GA, Perlow LA (2001) Taking time to integrate temporal research. Acad Manag Rev 26(4):512–529

Andrade GM, Mitchell ML, Stafford E (2001) New evidence and perspectives on mergers. Harvard Business School Working paper, No. 01-070. http://ssrn.com/abstract=269313

André P, Khalil S, Magnan M (2007) Termination fees in mergers and acquisitions: protecting investors or managers? J Bus Financ Account 34(3–4):541–566

Barkema HG, Schijven M (2008) Toward unlocking the full potential of acquisitions. Acad Manag J 51(4):696–722

Barkema H, Bell J, Pennings JME (1996) Foreign entry, cultural barriers and learning. Strateg Manag J 17(2):151–166

Bates TW, Lemmon ML (2003) Breaking up is hard to do? An analysis of termination fee provisions and merger outcomes. J Financ Econ 69(3):469–504

Berkovitch E, Narayanan MP (1993) Motives for takeovers: an empirical investigation. J Financ Quant Anal 28(3):347–362

Bert A, MacDonald T, Herd T (2003) Two merger integration imperatives: urgency and execution. Strateg Leadersh 31(3):42–49

Birkinshaw J, Bresman H, Håkanson L (2000) Managing the post-acquisition integration process: how the human iintegration and task integration processes interact to foster value creation. J Manag Stud 37(3):395–425

Bruner RF (2004) Deals from hell: M&A lessons that rise above the ashes. Wiley, New York, NY

Buono AF, Bowditch JL (1989) The human side of Mergers and acquisitions. Jossey-Bass, San Francisco, CA

Capron L, Pistre N (2002) When do acquirers earn abnormal returns? Strateg Manag J 23 (9):781–794

Capron L, Shen J (2007) Acquisition of private vs. public firms: private information, target selection, and acquirer returns. Strateg Manag J 28(9):891–911

Capron L, Dussauge P, Mitchell W (1998) Resource redeployment following horizontal acquisitions in Europe and North America 1988-1992. Strateg Manag J 19(7):631–661

Cartwright S, Cooper CL (1993) The psychological impact of merger and acquisition on the individual: a study of building society managers. Hum Relat 46:327–347
Cartwright S, Cooper CL (1996) Managing mergers, acquisitions, and strategic alliances: integrating people and cultures. Butterworth-Heinemann, Oxford
Cartwright S, Schoenberg R (2006) Thirty years of mergers and acquisitions research: recent advances and future opportunities. Br J Manag 17(S1):s1–s5
Chatterjee S (1992) Sources of value in takeovers: synergy or restructuring-implications for target and bidder firms. Strateg Manag J 13(4):267–286
Colombo G, Conca V, Buongiorno M, Gnan L (2007) Integrating cross-border acquisitions: a process-oriented approach. Long Range Plan 40(2):202–222
Copeland T (1994) Why value value? McKinsey Q 4:97–109
Cording M, Christmann P, King DR (2008) Reducing causal ambiguity in acquisition integration: intermediate goals as mediators of integration decisions and acquisition performance. Acad Manag J 51(4):744–767
Cullinan G, Le Roux J, Weddigen R (2004) When to walk away from a deal. Harv Bus Rev 82 (4):96–105
Cummings JL, Holmberg SR (2012) Best-fit Alliance partners: the use of critical success factors in a comprehensive partner selection process. Long Range Plan 45(2–3):136–159
Damodaran A (2005) The value of synergy. Stern School of Business, New York, NY. Available at SSRN 841486(2005). October 30
Datta DK (1991) Organizational fit and acquisition performance: effects of post-acquisition integration. Strateg Manag J 12(4):281–297
David K, Singh H (1994) Sources of acquisition cultural risk. In: Von Krogh G, Sinatra A, Singh H (eds) The management of corporate acquisitions. Macmillan, London, pp 251–292
Demirakos EG, Strong N, Walker M (2004) What valuation models do analysts use? Account Horiz 18(4):221–240
Devos E, Kadapakkam P, Krishnamurthy S (2009) A comparison of taxes, market power, and efficiency improvements as explanations for synergies. Rev Financ Stud 22(3):1179–1211
Duck JD (1993) Managing change: the art of balancing. Harv Bus Rev 71(6):109–118
Eccles RG, Lanes KL, Wilson TC (1999) Are you paying too much for that acquisition? Harv Bus Rev 77(4):136–146
Evans FC, Bishop DM (2001) Valuation for M&A: building value in private companies. Wiley, New York, NY
Fiorentino R, Garzella S (2015a) Synergy pitfalls management in mergers and acquisitions. Manag Decis 53(7):1469–1501
Fiorentino R, Garzella S (2015b) The synergy valuation models: towards the real value of mergers and acquisitions. Int Res J Financ Econ 124:71–82
Galpin TJ, Herndon M (2000) The complete guide to mergers and acquisitions: process tools to support M&A integration at every level. Wiley, New York, NY
Garzella S (2006) Il governo delle sinergie. Giappichelli, Torino
Garzella S, Fiorentino R (2014) A synergy measurement model to support the pre-deal decision making in mergers and acquisitions. Manag Decis 52(6):1194–1216
Gates S (2006) Incorporating strategic risk into enterprise risk management: a survey of current corporate practice. J Appl Corp Financ 18(4):81–90
Goold M, Campbell A (1998) Desperately seeking synergy. Harv Bus Rev 76:131–143
Goold M, Campbell A (2000) Taking stock of synergy. A framework for assessing linkages between business. Long Range Plan 33:72–96
Goold M, Quinn JJ (1990) Strategic control. Milestones for long-term performance. The Economist Books, Hutchinson
Gupta D, Gerchak Y (2002) Quantifying operational synergies in a merger/acquisition. Manag Sci 18:517–533
Haleblian J, Finkelstein S (1999) The influence of organizational acquisition experience on acquisition performance: a behavioral learning perspective. Admin Sci Q 44(1):29–56

Hambrick DC, Cannella AA (1993) Relative standing: a framework for understanding departures of acquired executives. Acad Manag J 36(4):733–762
Hammond JS, Keeney RL, Raiffa H (1998) The hidden traps in decision making. Harv Bus Rev 76 (5):47–58
Harding D, Rovit S (2005) Mastering the merger: four critical decisions that make or break the deal. Harvard Business School Press, Boston, MA
Haspeslagh PC, Jemison DB (1991) Managing acquisitions. Free Press, New York, NY
Haunschild PR, Beckmann CM (1998) When do interlocks matter? Alternate source of information and interlock influence. Admin Sci Q 43:815–844
Haunschild PR, Miner AS (1997) Modes of interorganizational imitation: the effects of outcome salience and uncertainty. Admin Sci Q 42(3):472–500
Hayward MLA (2002) When do firms learn from their acquisition experience? Evidence from 1990-1995. Strateg Manag J 23(1):21–39
Hill CWL, Hitt MA, Hoskisson RE (1992) Cooperative versus competitive structures in related and unrelated diversified firms. Organ Sci 3(4):501–521
Hitt MA, Dacin MT, Levitas E, Arregle JL, Borza A (2000) Partner selection in emerging and developed market contexts: resource-based and organizational learning perspectives. Acad Manag J 43(3):449–467
Hitt M, King D, Krishnan H, Makri M, Schijven K, Zhu H (2009) Mergers and acquisitions: overcoming pitfalls, building synergy, and creating value. Bus Horiz 52(6):523–529
Houston JF, James CM, Ryngaert MD (2001) Where do merger gains come from? Bank mergers from the perspective of insiders and outsiders. J Financ Econ 60(2–3):285–331
Hunt JW (1990) Changing pattern of acquisition behaviour in takeovers and the consequences for acquisition processes. Strateg Manag J 11(1):69–77
Kaplan S, Mitchell M, Wruck K (2000) A clinical exploration of value creation and destruction in acquisitions: integration, organization design, and internal capital markets. In: Kaplan S (ed) Mergers and productivity. National Bureau of Economic Research, Cambridge, MA
King DR, Dalton DR, Daily CD, Covin JG (2004) Meta-analyses of post-acquisition performance: indications of unidentified moderators. Strateg Manag J 25(2):187–200
Kotter JP (1995) Leading change. Why transformation efforts fail. Harv Bus Rev 85(2):59–87
KPMG (1999) Unlocking shareholder value: the keys to success. KPMG, London
Kroll M, Caples S (1987) Managing acquisitions of strategic business units with the aid of the arbitrage pricing model. Acad Manag Rev 12(4):676–685
Laarson R (1990) Coordination of action in mergers and acquisitions. Interpretative and system approaches towards synergy. Lund University Press, Lund
Larsson R, Finkelstein S (1999) Integrating strategic, organizational, and human resource perspectives on mergers and acquisitions: a case survey of synergy realization. Organ Sci 10 (1):1–26
Lorange P, Vancil RF (1977) Strategic planning system. Prentice Hall, Englewood Cliffs, NJ
Lubatkin M, O'Neill HM (1987) Merger strategies and capital market risk. Acad Manag J 30 (4):665–684
Marks ML, Mirvis PH (2000) Managing mergers, acquisitions, and alliances: creating an effective transition structure. Organ Dyn 28(3):35–47
Martinius P (2005) M&A: protecting the purchaser. Kluwer, Hague
Mathur SS, Kenyon A (1998) Creating value. Shaping tomorrow's business. Butterwoth-Heinemann, Oxford
McLaughlin R (1992) Investment-banking contracts in tender offers. J Financ Econ 28:209–232
Mukherjee TK, Kiymaz H, Baker K (2004) Merger motives and target valuation: a survey of evidence from CFOs. J Appl Financ 14(2):7–24
Nadler DA (2004) Building better boards. Harv Bus Rev 82:102–112
Nahavandi A, Malekzadeh AR (1988) Acculturation in mergers and acquisitions. Acad Manag Rev 13(1):79–90
Officer MS (2003) Termination fees in mergers and acquisitions. J Financ Econ 69(3):431–467

Pablo A (1994) Determinants of acquisition integration level: a decision-making perspective. Acad Manag J 37(4):803–836
Porter ME (1980) Competitive strategy. Free Press, New York, NY
Porter ME (1987) From competitive advantage to corporate strategy. Harv Bus Rev 65(3):43–59
Porter Liebeskind J (2000) Internal capital markets: benefits, costs, and organizational arrangements. Organ Sci 11(1):58–76
Rappaport A (1986) Creating shareholder value: the new standard for business performance. Free Press, New York, NY
Rappaport A, Sirower ML (1999) Stock or cash? The trade-offs for buyers and sellers in mergers and acquisitions. Harv Bus Rev 77(6):147–158
Russo A, Perrini F (2006) The real cost of M&A advice. Eur Manag J 24(1):49–58
Saint-Onge H, Chatzkel J (2009) Beyond the deal: a revolutionary framework for successful mergers & acquisitions that achieve breakthrough performance gains. McGraw-Hill, New York, NY
Sales AL, Mirvis PH (1984) When cultures collide: issue in acquisitions. In: Kimberley J, Quinn R (eds) New futures: the challenge of managing corporate transitions. Dow-Jones, Irwin, Homewood
Schuler R, Jackson S (2001) HR Issues and activities in mergers and acquisitions. Eur Manag J 19 (3):239–253
Schweiger DM, Ivancevich JM, Frank R (1987) Power executive actions for managing human resources before and after acquisition. Acad Manag Exec 1(2):127–138
Schweizer L, Patzelt H (2012) Employee commitment in the post-acquisition integration process: the effect of integration speed and leadership. Scand J Manag 28(4):298–310
Seyhun HN (1990) Do bidder managers knowingly pay too much for target firms? J Bus 63 (4):439–464
Shelton LM (1988) Strategic business fits and corporate acquisitions: empirical evidence. Strateg Manag J 9(3):279–287
Shimuzu K, Hitt M, Vaidyanath D, Pisano V (2004) Theoretical foundations of cross-border mergers and acquisitions: a review of current research and recommendations for the future. J Int Manag 10:307–353
Shrivastava P (1986) Postmerger integration. J Bus Strateg 7(1):65–76
Sirower ML (1997) Synergy trap: how companies lose the acquisition game. Simon & Schuster, New York, NY
Sirower ML, Sahni S (2006) Avoiding the "synergy trap": practical guidance on M&A decisions for CEOs and boards. J Appl Corpo Financ 18(3):83–95
Stahl GK, Angwin DN, Very P, Gomes E, Weber Y, Tarba SY, Noorderhaven N, Benyamini H, Bouckenooghe D, Chreim S, Durand M, Hassett ME, Kokk G, Mendenhall ME, Mirc N, Miska C, Park KM, Reynolds N-S, Rouzies A, Sarala RM, Seloti SL, Søndergaard M, Yildiz HE (2013) Sociocultural integration in mergers and acquisitions: unresolved paradoxes and directions for future research. Thunderbird Int Bus Rev 55(4):333–356
Tanriverdi H, Venkatraman N (2005) Knowledge relatedness and the performance of multibusiness firms. Strateg Manag J 26(2):97–119
Teerikangas S, Very P (2006) The culture-performance relationship in M&A: from yes/no to how. Br J Manag 17:31–48
Uhlenbruck K, Hitt MA, Semadeni M (2006) Market value effects of acquisitions involving Internet firms: a resource based analysis. Strateg Manag J 27(10):899–913
Vaara E (2002) On the discursive construction of success/failure in narratives of post-merger integration. Organ Stud 23:211–248
Vaara E (2003) Post-acquisition integration as sensemaking: glimpses of ambiguity, confusion, hypocrisy, and politicization. J Manag Stud 40(4):859–894
Weber Y (2011) Managing mergers and acquisitions: Implementation and integration. Int Stud Manag Organ 41(3):3–8

Zhang Y, Zhou J, Zhou N (2007) Audit committee quality, auditor independence, and internal control weaknesses. J Account Public Policy 26(3):300–327

Zhou YM (2011) Synergy, coordination costs, and diversification choices. Strateg Manag J 32:624–639

Zollo M, Singh H (2004) Deliberate learning in corporate acquisitions: post-acquisition strategies and integration capability in U.S. bank mergers. Strateg Manag J 25(13):1233–1256

Zott C, Amit R (2010) Business model design: an activity system perspective. Long Range Plan 43:216–226

Chapter 5
Conclusions

Abstract This book advances the ongoing debate about the failure rate of mergers and acquisitions that has remained consistently intense and in doing answers to the call for a greater recognition of M&A processes (Cartwright and Schoenberg, Br J Manag 17:s1–s5, 2006). Moreover, we enrich the fragmented M&A literature and we provide strong insights and implications for managers' commitment to synergy (Haleblian et al., J Manag 35:469–502, 2009; Knudsen, The essential tension in the social sciences: between the "unification" and "fragmentation" trap, Edward Elgar, 2003).

Keywords M&A literature • Managerial implications • Decision-making • Synergy pitfalls • Framework

This book advances the ongoing debate about the failure rate of mergers and acquisitions that has remained consistently intense and in doing answers to the call for a greater recognition of M&A processes (Cartwright and Schoenberg 2006). Moreover, we enrich the fragmented M&A literature and we provide strong insights and implications for managers' commitment to synergy (Haleblian et al. 2009; Knudsen 2003).

This study investigates the synergy in M&A processes to respond to the need for a comprehensive view of synergy management. As far as we know, this is the first time that a comprehensive investigation of synergy management in mergers and acquisitions has been developed.

We contribute to the literature on decision-making processes in M&A by suggesting relevant issues that could affect deal closing in the due-diligence step and methods of facilitating the integration process (Birkinshaw et al. 2000; Colombo et al. 2007; Haspeslagh and Jemison 1991; Shrivastava 1986). By developing an in-depth categorization of the several values of synergy, our paper also makes a distinct contribution to the literature on M&A performance by recommending factors to analyze in the synergy-measurement process (Eccles et al. 1999; Devos et al. 2009; Garzella 2006; Zollo and Meier 2008). We shed light on synergy management as a relevant mediator of variance in M&A performance (King et al. 2004). Focusing on synergy pitfalls, we integrate the literature on M&A critical success factors by suggesting the opposite: failure factors (Gomes et al. 2013; Shelton 1988).

S. Garzella, R. Fiorentino, *Synergy Value and Strategic Management*,
Contributions to Management Science, DOI 10.1007/978-3-319-40671-8_5

By presenting a review of M&A studies, we suggest moving quickly from an ambiguous conceptualization of the problems in M&A deals to one that is more accurate (Larsson and Finkelstein 1999; Lietdka 1998; Sirower 1997; Zhou 2011). In detail, we first shows that synergy is a multi-faceted concept: there are many types of synergy and several mechanisms of synergy creation and realization. The M&A synergy literature has evolved from a focus on the nature and types of synergy to a more pragmatic focus on the measurement and assessment of synergy value (e.g., Chatterjee 1986; Sirower 1997; Garzella and Fiorentino 2014). Specifically, the literature review shows that over time, studies on synergy management can be systematized around three broad streams: (1) identification of the role of synergy in external growth strategies, which allows firms to identify synergy as an important motive for M&As; (2) analysis of synergy achievement in the M&A process, which highlights how difficult it is to realize synergy; and (3) the assessment of value creation in M&As, which pushes organizations to warn against "synergy trap". Each literature stream provides a relevant contribution to the development of a framework for synergy management pitfalls (Fiorentino and Garzella 2015a, b). The literature about M&A motives emphasizes relevant insights. Since it is useful to verify the existence of potential synergy, the synergy management may start from the pre-deal steps. Since the sources of potential synergy are based on either strategy or finance, the synergy assessment should analytically identify several values of synergy. Indeed, some synergy pitfalls might hide behind extra-synergy motives. The second area of investigation, M&A process, provides additional insights. Since the achievement of expected synergies is generally difficult, firms should estimate the difficulties and the integration costs in the pre-deal steps. The integration approach, according to the assessment of potential synergy and organizational difficulties, may be developed prior to concluding the deal. The assessment of difficulties may analyze many of the issues highlighted in the various literature streams. Moreover, the distinction between revenue growth and cost-saving synergies should be useful in the assessment process to identify potential difficulties at the integration stage. Consequently, the literature suggests the importance of the integration step. Furthermore, a lack of attention to organizational issues should be the cause of some other pitfalls. This issue imply adding organization fit to the strategic fit analysis (Stahl et al. 2013). The third literature stream, M&A value creation, suggests the relevance of synergy pitfalls. The existence of several causes implies the existence of multiple types of risk. However, studies reattach the risks of an unsuccessful synergy achievement to a single "trap". Research examining the several types of pitfalls that may hinder the success of M&A deals remains surprisingly limited (Goold and Campbell 1998; Hitt et al. 2009). Since risks are reattached to a single and generic trap, managers and advisors have been given little guidance on the specific causes of "synergy pitfalls" and on the most effective way to avoid them. Consequently, this gap requires the careful identification of the main types of synergy pitfalls by connecting each pitfall to the related cause and the most useful solutions.

We suggest to warn firms of the potential risks of inaccurate synergy estimations and, at the same time, suggest that an effective synergy assessment process have to be developed to increase the likelihood of M&A success. The process should embrace a quantitative evaluation of synergy value. Managers, advisors and consultants should give a preference for models based on "net present value" which have frequent use for synergy assessment. These preference is consistent with the results of prior research suggesting a change in preference in favour of sophisticated valuation models (Imam et al. 2008) and a preference for "net present value" models in mergers and acquisitions (Garzella and Fiorentino 2014; Mukherjee et al. 2004). However, other types of models, such as accounting models, are also used in practice (Demirakos et al. 2004). Indeed, there is widespread consensus on the simultaneous use of different models as control models, consistent with earlier research suggesting that valuation models are complementary to each other and more relevant in combination (Barker 1999). However, we highlight that the path preference and the forecasting process play significantly greater roles than the choice of the version of the model to use. All of the information on strategic factors affecting the synergy flows is very relevant. Specifically, firms should analyze four strategic factors affecting the synergy value: synergy form, synergy size, synergy timing and synergy likelihood. Based on these findings, we advance a model useful to support the pre-deal decision making. The measurement process should start from the analysis of synergy form. First, an examination of "what" is the synergy nature is useful, distinguishing operating synergies from financial and tax synergies and providing suitable sub-categorizations. A pure operating logic aiming to increase market power and the efficiency of manufacturing processes is the basis of operating synergies (Sirower 1997). Financial synergies are created to reduce financing costs by sharing financial resources and exploiting possible cash flow asynchronies between involved firms (Porter Liebeskind 2000). The final sub-category consists of tax synergies that aim to decrease taxation pressures on firms (Copeland 1994) by reducing the taxable income and the tax band. Second, executives should forecast "how" these synergies will arise with reference to the financial exhibition of synergistic flows. Each prior type or sub-type of synergy should produce higher revenues or lower costs. Third, the measurement process should clarify "where" synergistic flow may be allocated: at one SBU, at one division or at the corporate level. The organizational level of synergy allocation should help the observation and the measurement of synergy. Some synergies are most likely to occur at the corporate level more than within SBUs or "intermediate" divisions, which groups SBUs. On the contrary different synergies will be far fewer in number and more difficult to identify at the corporate level.

Since the assessment and the integration processes don't generally follow our suggested guidelines, there is a relevant risk of ineffective management in M&As. There are many pitfalls, and not a single trap, that could affect the synergy management that transforms a good M&A into a very bad deal (Hammond et al. 1998). The executives involved in M&A agreements have often underestimated the management of synergy pitfalls, and this lack of attention has substantially driven deal failure (Harding and Rovit 2005). Despite significant progress, the extant synergy management literature still suffers from several shortcomings. There is a lack of integration across research paths pertinent to the study of synergy management. We contribute to the existing literature by improving the analysis in the strategic management literature, considering and incorporating insights from new streams and the contiguous literature. Indeed, we answer to the call for further research about "how" to manage synergy pitfalls by developing a comprehensive framework that is useful for both scholars and practitioners.

In addition, we extend the existing body of knowledge by developing a framework aimed at supporting the management of synergy in mergers and acquisitions using a multi-dimensions perspective in a process approach (Hayward 2002; Larsson and Finkelstein 1999; Lietdka 1998; Zollo and Meier 2008). We analyze the "content" of synergy management by identifying the most relevant dimensions, we conceptualize the most relevant pitfalls, and we develop the "process" to pinpoint and avoid synergy pitfalls. In order to suggest the critical actions that firms can develop to manage synergy pitfalls, five perspectives must be analyzed: the management of synergy in the main step of the M&A process; the analysis of the several values of synergy; the recognition of the forbidding effects of improper synergy management; the evaluation of the potential causes of synergy trap; and the selection of the potential solutions to synergy pitfalls. These dimensions show "when", "where", "what", "why" and "how" to manage synergy pitfalls, leading firms to improve the M&A success rate. The framework exploits the generic notion of "synergy trap" in the three most analytical and useful concepts of synergyy pitfalls. The mirage is a tendency to overestimate synergy potential. The "gravity hill" is the danger of underestimating the difficulties of synergy realization. The "amnesia" is a dangerous lack of attention to the synergy realization process. Despite prior studies, our framework enables firms to become better equipped to address synergy challenge in a comprehensive manner. To verify the existence of potential synergy, it is useful to refer to partner-selection studies and findings. To effectively assess synergy value, firms should use appropriate synergy measurement models. Indeed, to fully achieve the expected synergy, firms should adopt a change-management approach. Starting from these guidelines, we integrate behaviors, actions and tools developed in several literature streams and we provide guidelines to select the right solutions with respect to each pitfall.

This finding suggests that firms should integrate workers and tools from different backgrounds, from strategy to accounting, to effectively assess the synergy value, consistent with the call for cooperation between strategy, accounting and valuation (Damodaran 2005).

Following the guidelines of our model, we also propose a synergy statement in response to the needs of practitioners for best practices in pre-deal decision making. The use of the suggested synergy statement could facilitate the pre-acquisition decision process that indicates which acquisitions are "right".

Finally, we suggest that future research on synergy in M&As should integrate all of the relevant literature streams. More specifically, scholars should analyze the connections among merging firm selection studies, synergy measurement models and integration process issues. Studies on assessment and measurement issues (Colombo et al. 2007), generally focused on pre-deal steps, should be extended to the integration process. Similarly, research on organizational issues (Vaara 2003), typically focused on the integration process, should be integrated into the pre-deal studies. Indeed, useful insights to practitioners could arise out of research testing the impact on the M&A performance of suggested solutions to synergy pitfalls. Otherwise, analysis of the features of M&A teams and merging firms' boards should provide useful validation for people with different backgrounds.

References

Barker RG (1999) The role of dividends in valuation models used by analysts and fund managers. Eur Account Rev 8(2):195–218

Birkinshaw J, Bresman H, Håkanson L (2000) Managing the post-acquisition integration process: how the human integration and task integration processes interact to foster value creation. J Manag Stud 37(3):395–425

Cartwright S, Schoenberg R (2006) Thirty years of mergers and acquisitions research: recent advances and future opportunities. Br J Manag 17(S1):s1–s5

Chatterjee S (1986) Types of synergy and economic value: the impact of acquisitions on merging and rival firms. Strateg Manag J 7(2):119–139

Colombo G, Conca V, Buongiorno M, Gnan L (2007) Integrating cross-border acquisitions: a process-oriented approach. Long Range Plan 40(2):202–222

Copeland T (1994) Why Value Value? McKinsey Q 4:97–109

Damodaran A (2005) The value of synergy. Stern School of Business, New York, NY

Demirakos EG, Strong N, Walker M (2004) What valuation models do analysts use? Account Horiz 18(4):221–240

Devos E, Kadapakkam P, Krishnamurthy S (2009) A comparison of taxes, market power, and efficiency improvements as explanations for synergies. Rev Financ Stud 22(3):1179–1211

Eccles RG, Lanes KL, Wilson TC (1999) Are you paying too much for that acquisition? Harv Bus Rev 77(4):136–146

Fiorentino R, Garzella S (2015a) Synergy pitfalls management in mergers and acquisitions. Manag Decis 53(7):1469–1501

Fiorentino R, Garzella S (2015b) The synergy valuation models: towards the real value of mergers and acquisitions. Int Res J Financ Econ 124:71–82

Garzella S (2006) Il governo delle sinergie. Giappichelli, Torino

Garzella S, Fiorentino R (2014) A synergy measurement model to support the pre-deal decision making in mergers and acquisitions. Manag Decis 52(6):1194–1216

Gomes E, Angwin DN, Weber Y, Tarba SY (2013) Critical success factors through the mergers and acquisitions process: revealing pre- and post-M&A connections for improved performance. Thunderbird Int Bus Rev 55(1):13–35

Goold M, Campbell A (1998) Desperately seeking synergy. Harv Bus Rev 76:131–143

Haleblian J, Devers C, McNamara G, Carpenter M, Davison R (2009) Taking stock of what we know about mergers and acquisitions: a review and research agenda. J Manag 35(3):469–502

Hammond JS, Keeney RL, Raiffa H (1998) The hidden traps in decision making. Harv Bus Rev 76 (5):47–58

Harding D, Rovit S (2005) Mastering the merger: four critical decisions that make or break the deal. Harvard Business School Press, Boston, MA

Haspeslagh PC, Jemison DB (1991) Managing acquisitions. Free Press, New York, NY

Hayward MLA (2002) When do firms learn from their acquisition experience? Evidence from 1990-1995. Strateg Manag J 23(1):21–39

Hitt M, King D, Kriishnan H, Makri M, Schijven K, Zhu H (2009) Mergers and acquisitions: overcoming pitfalls, building synergy, and creating value. Bus Horiz 52(6):523–529

Imam S, Barker R, Clubb C (2008) The use of valuation models by UK Investment Analysts. Eur Account Rev 17(3):503–535

King DR, Dalton DR, Daily CD, Covin JG (2004) Meta-analyses of post-acquisition performance: indications of unidentified moderators. Strateg Manag J 25(2):187–200

Knudsen C (2003) The essential tension in the social sciences: between the "unification" and "fragmentation" trap. Edward Elgar, Cheltenham, England

Larsson R, Finkelstein S (1999) Integrating strategic, organizational, and human resource perspectives on mergers and acquisitions: a case survey of synergy realization. Organ Sci 10 (1):1–26

Lietdka JM (1998) Synergy revisited: how a "Screwball Buzzword" can be good for the bottom line. Bus Strateg Rev 9(2):45–55

Mukherjee TK, Kiymaz H, Baker K (2004) Merger motives and target valuation: a survey of evidence from CFOs. J Appl Financ 14(2):7–24

Porter Liebeskind J (2000) Internal capital markets: benefits, costs, and organizational arrangements. Organ Sci 11(1):58–76

Shelton LM (1988) Strategic business fits and corporate acquisitions: empirical evidence. Strateg Manag J 9(3):279–287

Shrivastava P (1986) Postmerger integration. J Bus Strategy 7(1):65–76

Sirower ML (1997) Synergy trap: how companies lose the acquisition game. Simon & Schuster, New York, NY

Stahl GK, Angwin DN, Very P, Gomes E, Weber Y, Tarba SY, Noorderhaven N, Benyamini H, Bouckenooghe D, Chreim S, Durand M, Hassett ME, Kokk G, Mendenhall ME, Mirc N, Miska C, Park KM, Reynolds N-S, Rouzies A, Sarala RM, Seloti SL, Søndergaard M, Yildiz HE (2013) Sociocultural integration in mergers and acquisitions: unresolved paradoxes and directions for future research. Thunderbird Int Bus Rev 55(4):333–356

Vaara E (2003) Post-acquisition Integration as sensemaking: glimpses of ambiguity, confusion, hypocrisy, and politicization. J Manag Stud 40(4):859–894

Zhou YM (2011) Synergy, coordination costs, and diversification choices. Strateg Manag J 32:624–639

Zollo M, Meier D (2008) What Is M&A performance? Acad Manag Perspect 22(3):55–77

Index

S. Garzella, R. Fiorentino, *Synergy Value and Strategic Management*, Contributions to Management Science, DOI 10.1007/978-3-319-40671-8

The manufacturer's authorised representative in the EU is Springer Nature Customer Service Centre GmbH, Europaplatz 3, 69115 Heidelberg, Germany. If you have any concerns regarding our products, please contact ProductSafety@springernature.com

Printed and bound by CPI Group (UK) Ltd, Croydon, CR0 4YY
30/09/2026
02225666-0020